JAMES McNAIR's
SALADS

Photography by
Jim Hildreth and James McNair

Chronicle Books • San Francisco

Printed in Singapore

Library of Congress
Cataloging-in-Publication Data
McNair, James K.
[Salads]
James McNair's Salads
/Photography by Jim Hildreth
and James McNair.
p. cm.
Includes index.
ISBN 0-87701-825-1
ISBN 0-87701-819-7 (pbk.)
1. Salada I. Hildreth, Jim. II. Title.
TX740.M35 1991
641.8'3—dc20   91-8522
                        CIP

Distributed in Canada by
Raincoast Books
8680 Cambie Street
Vancouver, B.C. V6P 6M9

10 9 8 7 6 5

Chronicle Books
85 Second Street
San Francisco, CA 94105

Web Site: www.chronbooks.com

For the people at Chronicle Books who are responsible for making my book series such a success. To former Publisher Larry Smith, who saw my potential and bought *Cold Pasta* when other publishers were turning down all my ideas. To Jack Jensen, current Publisher and guiding force behind the phenomenal growth of the company, who always listens to my woes and offers sage counsel. To Senior Editor Bill LeBlond, who has overseen all of my Chronicle books, and to Editor-in-Chief Nion McEvoy and Managing Editor Annie Barrows, whose kid-glove treatment makes my work go smoothly. To Marketing Director Drew Montgomery, Sales Director Julie Chanter, Foreign Rights and Book Club Sales Director Betsy Foster, Promotions Manager Janet Saevitz, and Associate Promotions Manager Sally Barrows for guiding the tremendous upsurge in sales. To Publicity Director Mary Ann Gilderbloom for promoting my name and my books. To Art Director Karen Pike, Senior Designer Julie Noyes Long and Production Manager Nancy Reid for maintaining such high quality in the printing of my work. To Controller Laura Baldwin who keeps royalty payments prompt. And to all the assistants and business personnel who keep everything flowing so smoothly.

Produced by The Rockpile Press, San Francisco and Lake Tahoe

Art direction, photographic design, prop and food styling, and book design by James McNair

Editorial and photographic production assistance by Lin Cotton

Editorial, styling, and photographic assistance by Ellen Berger-Quan

Typography and mechanical production by Cleve Gallat and Samantha Schwemler of CTA Graphics

CONTENTS

INTRODUCTION   4

SALADS   7

DRESSINGS & TOPPINGS   79

INDEX   94

ACKNOWLEDGMENTS   96

INTRODUCTION

Probably no menu item has matured as fully as the salad during America's recent culinary revolution. I was almost grown before I realized that the salad course didn't automatically mean sweet gelatin molds, which still serve that purpose on many tables in the Deep South. Admittedly, some of these old-fashioned concoctions are delicious as side dishes and desserts, but they are a long way from what I now think of as crisp, refreshing salads.

Back in the salad days of my youth, we also ate wedges of iceberg lettuce smothered with thick, and again usually sweet, orange "French" or pickle-laced Thousand Island dressing. Such a heavy mask was needed to add flavor to the bland but crisp lettuce. Potato salads and coleslaws showed up regularly, too, especially at barbecues, fish fries, and church dinner-on-the-grounds.

Upon moving to New Orleans in the 1960s, I expanded my greens repertoire with mixed Italian salad, which added romaine lettuce to the iceberg and threw in olives, tomatoes, artichokes, anchovies, and one or two cooked vegetables. This mix still miraculously survives in the Crescent City, even in households and restaurants of Italian descent, as the disparagingly named wop salad.

The origin of the word salad is the Latin *sal,* or "salt." Its adoption is believed to have grown out of the ancient Roman habit of dipping greens in salt before eating them.

Today salad reaches far beyond that narrow definition. Almost any ingredient can be turned into a salad, which in turn may be served chilled, warm, at room temperature, or even in a combination of temperatures, such as chilled crisp greens topped with slices of warm meat or fish. Salads no longer only begin a meal or follow the main course. They may very well serve as satisfying entrées. Nor are they merely thought of as diet food, although they can be among the best dishes to eat when you need to lose a few pounds. That's because they are usually rich in fiber and nutrients and, with attention to lighter dressing, can be low in calories. In fact, a robust salad can also be a complete, well-balanced meal all on its own.

Ideas and ingredients from around the world have been added to our salad repertoire. In this book, I have included several of my favorite salads from Southeast Asia. Versatile eggplant goes international with three versions—Asian, Middle Eastern, and Mediterranean. I enjoy mixing cuisines, too: Western-style tossed greens are dressed with a vinaigrette made from Far Eastern staples, and American coleslaw is paired with an Asian-style peanut dressing.

Many of the presentations in this book are composed salads, in which the components are attractively arranged on individual plates or on a large platter instead of tossed together. In such compositions, ingredients are frequently grouped atop a bed of greens. You may also serve small portions of several different salads on a single plate as a sampler; choose those with compatible flavors and offer a range of textures from crisp to soft.

While small portions can serve as starters, accompaniments, or refreshers after a main course, most salads can easily be expanded to become the centerpiece of the meal. The emphasis of this book is on main-dish salads. Even when recipes don't appear to be substantial enough to satisfy most people as an entrée, check the introductory comments for ideas on how to enhance the dish.

My salad collection begins with basic tossed greens and ends with fruit salads that can double as desserts. In between are mixes of a cornucopia of vegetables, as well as salads featuring grains, seafood, poultry, or meats. The final section of the book presents dozens of vinaigrettes and other dressings and garnishes that are called for in the salad recipes. Here you'll also find suggestions for other ways to use the dressings. I hope that the recipes and ideas in this book inspire you to create your own unique salad combinations, an important goal of every good cookbook.

SALADS

Basic Green Salad

The days are past when a green salad meant ubiquitous iceberg, the once exotic romaine, or the occasional limestone or butter lettuce. A vast array of "designer" greens sold in many markets or grown in our gardens allows us to compose everyday salads that are picture perfect. See the following two pages for greens suggestions. Now there is also a wide range of oils, vinegars, and seasonings for dressing salads that were unheard of by most home cooks until recent years.

Some purists still insist that a tossed salad should be composed of only greens; others enjoy combining chunks of tomatoes, cucumbers, onions, or other vegetables with the leafy components. For my own house salad, I prefer to stick with a mixture of tender greens, including sprigs of fresh herbs, unless I have some very flavorful seasonal tomatoes to add. Occasionally I will dress up a green salad with some sliced seasonal fruit or a sprinkle of toasted nuts, seeds, or freshly grated Parmesan cheese.

Wash, dry, and chill the greens as described on page 10.

Prepare the vinaigrette and set aside.

Just before serving the salad, place the greens in a large bowl and pour on the dressing to taste; do not overdress. (The greens should be lightly coated, never soggy.) Serve immediately. Alternatively, arrange the greens on individual plates and drizzle the dressing over the top or pass it at the table.

Serves 6 as a salad course.

12 cups small whole or torn salad greens, one kind or a combination (pages 10 and 11)
Basic Vinaigrette (page 80) or any variation (pages 81 and 82)

SALAD GREENS

CLEANING AND CRISPING

Greens can either stand on their own as a salad or act as a base heartier salad. In either case they should be thoroughly cleaned, completely dried, and well chilled.

Separate greens into individual leaves. If the leaves are large, tear them into bite-sized pieces either before washing or just before serving. Remove tough lower stems from watercress, cilantro (coriander), mint, parsley, or other stalky herbs; separate basil or mint into individual leaves, if desired. Wash the greens under running cold water. Or fill a basin with cold water, immerse the greens, and agitate the greens in the water to rinse well. Allow any grit or soil to settle to the bottom of the basin, then remove the greens. Drain off the water and repeat the process until the water is clear.

Transfer the wet greens to a salad spinner and spin to remove as much water as possible. Pat dry with paper toweling. Alternatively, wrap the greens in a cloth towel and shake vigorously to remove moisture; pat dry with paper toweling.

Wrap the dried greens in a clean cloth towel or in paper toweling and refrigerate for at least 30 minutes or for up to several hours to crisp. For longer storage, place the wrapped greens in a large plastic bag or plastic storage container and refrigerate for up to 3 days.

As one who grew up during the heyday of iceberg lettuce, spinach, and cabbage salads, I'm delighted to see the recent expansion in the choice of salad greens offered by many markets. The supermarkets and specialty produce stores where I shop have spoiled me by offering premixed young greens, what the French call *mesclun,* although I sometimes prefer to purchase specific greens and mix them with my homegrown herbs, edible blossoms, or baby greens.

When your produce market can't or won't bother to supply greens other than the long-lasting old standbys, grow your own greens from seeds offered by numerous garden catalogs or pick up seedlings at a good nursery.

LETTUCE. Ubiquitous supermarket **iceberg** is best left for salads or other dishes that require crispness but not much flavor. **Romaine**, also called **Cos**, tastes slightly nutty and sweet when young; unfortunately supermarkets stock huge mature heads and only the pale inner leaves are worth eating. Subtly sweet leaves of **Bibb** lettuce, also known as **limestone**, and **butter**, which is sometimes called **Boston** lettuce, are loosely folded into soft delicate heads that make shipping and storage difficult; these varieties are worth finding a good source for or growing your own. Delicate-tasting **leaf lettuces** that do not form obvious heads have frilled or crumpled edges and may be all green or bordered in red or brownish red. **Oak leaf** lettuce is one example.

BITTER CHICORY. Frilly-edged leaves of **curly chicory**, also known as **curly endive,** form a flat head. **Frisée** is a type of French curly endive that is smaller and more delicate than its heartier relative. **Escarole**, also known as **broad-leafed** or **batavian endive**, has larger, looser leaves. Pricey **Belgian endive** grows from witloof chicory, the root of which is used as an addition to or substitute for coffee. The tender endive shoots are formed when the plant is covered with soil and kept in darkness. The tubular-shaped heads are composed of tightly bunched, cream-colored leaves that are tinged with green at the top and have a bitter taste. Ruby-hued, white-veined leaves of **radicchio** varieties form compact heads.

OTHER ASSERTIVE GREENS. The dark green, notched leaves of **arugula**, also called **rocket cress**, **roquette**, and **rugula**, have a sharp peppery flavor reminiscent of other relatives in the mustard family. **Garden cress**, which also goes by the names **curly cress** and **pepper grass**, resembles parsley in appearance and tastes peppery, like its cousin, **watercress**, which grows in shallow moving water. Long, slender, indented **dandelion** leaves, considered too-familiar lawn pests by some, are prized for their tart taste by others. Sprigs or leaves of fresh herbs add considerable interest to salad greens; add only one kind or a taste-pleasing combination. In green salads, I particularly enjoy **chervil**, **chives**, **cilantro** or **coriander**, **basil**, **lemon balm**, **lemon thyme**, **mint**, **parsley**, **savory**, and **tarragon**. The dark green, elongated leaves of **sorrel**, or **French sorrel**, are lemon flavored. Spicy, green **radish** seedlings add zestiness to salads.

ASIAN GREENS. **Garland chrysanthemum**, or **shungiku**, looks like chrysanthemum foliage. Although strongly flavored, the young leaves have no bitterness or tartness. **Bok choy**, or **Chinese mustard cabbage**, is a nonheading cabbage with thick stalks. Pungent **mizuna** is a Japanese relative of the mustard family.

CABBAGE. Familiar round, compact heads in red or pale green are crisp and strong flavored. Also try **savoy,** with its bright green, crinkled leaves, and the delicately flavored, elongated **Chinese** or **celery varieties**, such as creamy white, green-tinged **Napa**.

GREENS. Tender young leaves of **beet**, **chard**, **kale**, **mustard**, and **turnip** make delicious salad additions. Uniquely flavored deep green **spinach** normally grows in cool weather and tastes best when young and tender; warm weather spinach varieties include vinelike **Malabar** and low-growing **New Zealand spinach**.

WILD GREENS. Originally gathered in the wilds but now under cultivation, little round leaves of **mâche**, also known as **corn salad**, **field lettuce**, and **lamb's lettuce**, have a mild, nutty taste. The leaves of **miner's lettuce**, sometimes called **winter purslane** or **Indian lettuce**, taste similar to watercress and are shaped like shallow bowls, with flowers sprouting from the center. Crunchy and nutty-tasting **fiddleheads** are young and succulent unfurled fern fronds.

SERVING WARE

Some people like to serve and eat salads from bowls. I generally prefer to present beautifully arranged salad greens or other components in an attractive salad bowl, toss them at the table, and then serve the salad on plates, or occasionally in handsome bowls. When I serve composed salads, I either arrange them ahead of time in the kitchen on individual salad or dinner plates, or assemble all the components in a pleasing design on large platters for serving or passing at the table. No matter which style you choose, prechilled plates and forks always add a nice touch when serving crisp greens.

Bowls for tossing or serving salads come in a mind-boggling array of materials, sizes, and colors. Except for vessels made of metals or those with metallic glazes that could react with acidic dressings, almost any plate can be used for serving salads. Don't confine salads to salad plates; some arrangements need the extra space of dinner plates or even buffet plates or chargers.

I've read in countless sources that wooden salad bowls should be merely wiped out, never washed. But oils turn rancid and their residue should be thoroughly washed away after use. Choose wooden salad bowls or plates that have been sealed and waterproofed, so that they may be washed between uses.

Caesar Salad with Garlic Croutons

Since its inception in a Tijuana restaurant, this classic has never gone completely out of favor. Recent years have even seen a resurgence of its popularity in America's trendsetting restaurants.

I prefer to leave the lettuce leaves whole, to be picked up with the fingertips for nibbling. If you would rather use a fork, break the leaves before tossing them with the dressing. Even though tradition dictates mixing the dressing in a wooden bowl before adding the lettuce, I like to make the dressing separately. That way there is more control over the amount of dressing that ends up tossed with the greens.

Eggs may contain dangerous bacteria that are only killed once the white and yolk are firmly set. If the eggs in your area have this problem, the dressing may be made without the traditional coddled egg; a drizzle of heavy cream will add the richness normally provided by the egg.

Wash, dry, and chill the lettuce leaves as described on page 10.

Prepare the Croutons and set aside.

Just before serving the salad, prepare the dressing. Bring a small pot of water to a rapid boil over high heat. Place the eggs, one at a time, on a spoon, lower them into the boiling water, and boil for 1 minute. Transfer the eggs to cold water to cool. Break the eggs, separating the yolks into a small bowl; discard the whites. Add the anchovy fillets, garlic, mustard, oil, and about half of the lemon juice to the yolks and whisk to blend. Whisk in the remaining lemon juice, or more to taste, and salt, and pepper to taste.

In a large bowl, combine the whole lettuce leaves, about half of the croutons, and half of the cheese. Add the dressing to taste and toss well. Arrange the salad on a serving platter or individual plates. Sprinkle with the remaining croutons and cheese and serve immediately. Pass a pepper mill at the table.

Serves 10 to 12 as a salad course, or 6 to 8 as a light main course.

4 medium-sized heads romaine lettuce, tough outer leaves discarded, separated into about 48 leaves
4 cups Croutons (page 92), made with plenty of garlic

CAESAR DRESSING
3 eggs
6 flat anchovy fillets, drained and minced
1 tablespoon minced or pressed garlic
2 teaspoons Dijon-style mustard
1 cup fruity olive oil, preferably extra-virgin
About 3 tablespoons freshly squeezed lemon juice
About ¼ teaspoon salt
About 1 teaspoon freshly ground black pepper
½ cup freshly shredded Parmesan cheese, preferably parmigiano-reggiano
Freshly ground black pepper for serving

Fruit, Nuts, and Greens Salad

The pairing of crisp greens with sliced fruit and sprinkled with toasted nuts is a new American classic with many variations. I usually serve a combination of watercress, pecans, apples, and cranberries or blueberries on a Thanksgiving dinner menu or for other autumn meals. Pears, walnuts, and Belgian endives, another popular combo, are frequently teamed with chunks of blue cheese and tossed in Walnut Vinaigrette (page 82). For an offbeat trio, mix spinach, sliced bananas, and walnuts in Creamy Vinaigrette (page 81) made with evaporated milk. As an elegant autumn opener or main course, combine julienned apples and shredded Belgian endives, top with smoked or grilled quail (if desired), sprinkle with fresh pomegranate seeds and toasted macadamia nuts, and drizzle with Basic Vinaigrette (page 80).

Wash, dry, and chill the greens as described on page 10.

Prepare the nuts and set aside.

Prepare the vinaigrette and set aside.

Just before serving, quarter the apples or pears lengthwise and core them. Thinly slice the quarters into a bowl. Add the lemon juice and stir well to keep the fruit from discoloring.

In a salad bowl, combine the greens, toasted nuts, apple or pear slices, and berries. Pour the vinaigrette to taste over the salad and toss thoroughly. Serve immediately.

Serves 6 to 8 as a salad course or accompaniment.

About 8 cups small whole or torn salad greens, one kind or a combination (pages 10 and 11)
1 cup coarsely chopped Sweet Crunchy Nuts (page 90) or Oven-Toasted Nuts (page 90)
Berry Vinaigrette (page 81)
3 medium-sized apples or pears
About 2 tablespoons freshly squeezed lemon juice
1 cup fresh berries (same kind as used in Vinaigrette)

Peanutty Coleslaw

1 head cabbage (about 1½ pounds)
3 tablespoons rice vinegar or white wine vinegar
2 tablespoons freshly squeezed lemon juice
⅓ cup Asian-style sesame oil
⅓ cup smooth peanut butter, at room temperature
1 cup Mayonnaise (page 85) or high-quality commercial real mayonnaise
1 tablespoon soy sauce
About 1 teaspoon salt
About 2 teaspoons freshly ground black pepper
About 1 teaspoon hot chile oil
1 tablespoon unsalted butter
1 cup unsalted roasted peanuts
Pesticide-free edible flowers such as borage, dianthus, or nasturtium for garnish (optional)

Outstanding with barbecued or grilled meats, especially baby back ribs, this slaw tastes best when prepared a few hours before serving. If made ahead and refrigerated, however, be sure to bring it back to room temperature before serving.

Any variety of cabbage (page 11) may be used alone or combined with different types for some diversity in color and flavor. I like to serve the slaw nestled inside a collar made from the leaves of savoy cabbage or colorful edible kale.

Discard any wilted outer leaves of the cabbage. Rinse the head under cold running water. Using a food processor or a sharp knife, shred the cabbage and place it in a large bowl.

In a food processor or blender, combine the vinegar, lemon juice, sesame oil, peanut butter, Mayonnaise, and soy sauce. Blend well. Season to taste with salt, pepper, and chile oil. Pour the vinegar mixture over the cabbage and toss thoroughly. Cover and let stand at room temperature for about 2 hours, or refrigerate for up to 24 hours. Return the coleslaw to room temperature before serving.

In a skillet, melt the butter over low heat. Add the peanuts and cook, stirring frequently, until the peanuts are golden brown and fragrant, about 3 minutes; watch carefully to prevent burning. Transfer to paper toweling to drain and cool.

Just before serving, stir in most of the peanuts, saving a few to sprinkle over the top. Garnish with flowers (if used).

Serves 8 as a salad course or accompaniment.

Eggplant Salad

This Mediterranean-inspired salad is shown with both Asian and Middle Eastern variations.

Wash, dry, and chill the lettuce leaves as described on page 10.

Place the salted eggplant slices in a colander, and let drain for about 30 minutes.

Prepare the vinaigrette and set aside.

Toast the nuts and set aside.

Blot the eggplant slices dry with paper toweling. In a sauté pan or skillet, pour in olive oil to cover barely the bottom of the pan. Add the eggplant slices, a few at a time, and cook until tender and lightly browned on both sides, about 10 minutes total; add olive oil as needed. Using a slotted utensil, transfer the eggplant to paper toweling to drain. Alternatively, brush the slices with the oil, spread on a baking sheet, and roast in a preheated 400° F oven, or grill over a moderate fire, until browned and tender, about 25 minutes.

In a salad bowl, combine the lettuce, eggplant, cheese, and toasted pine nuts and toss with the vinaigrette to taste. Serve immediately.

Serves 8 as a salad course, or 4 as a main course.

VARIATIONS: For an Asian-style salad, omit the lettuce, cheese, and nuts. Substitute Asian-Style Vinaigrette (page 81) for the Mustard Vinaigrette. Cut the eggplant into bite-sized pieces and stir- fry in about 2 tablespoons peanut oil in a wok or deep skillet until tender, about 5 minutes. Toss the eggplant with the vinaigrette and sprinkle with ½ cup pan-toasted sesame seeds (page 91) and ½ cup julienned green onion.

For a Middle Eastern-style salad, omit the lettuce, cheese, and pine nuts. Substitute 4 cups Nonfat Yogurt Dressing, Middle Eastern Variation (page 86) for the Mustard Vinaigrette. Toss with the cooked eggplant slices, cover, and refrigerate overnight. Bring to room temperature before serving and garnish with fresh mint sprigs.

2 heads butter lettuce or other tender lettuce
2 pounds globe eggplants, sliced crosswise about ¼ inch thick and sprinkled with 2 teaspoons coarse salt
Mustard Vinaigrette (page 81), made with Dijon-style mustard
½ cup pine nuts, pan toasted (page 91)
Fruity olive oil, preferably extra-virgin for sautéing, baking, or grilling
8 ounces goat's milk cheese or blue cheese, crumbled

Warm Wild Mushroom Salad

Top with bite-sized pieces of grilled, roasted, or sautéed duck, pheasant, or quail for a rich main course.

Wash, dry, and chill the greens as described on page 10.

Toast the nuts, chop coarsely, and set aside.

A few minutes before serving, arrange the greens on individual plates. In a sauté pan or skillet, combine the oils and warm over medium heat. Add the mushrooms and sauté, until just tender, 3 to 4 minutes. Remove from the heat and cool for about 1 minute. Stir in the vinegar and mustard and season to taste with salt. Spoon the mushrooms over the greens, sprinkle with the cheese and toasted nuts, and serve immediately. Pass a pepper mill at the table.

Serves 6 to 8 as a salad course, or 3 as a main course.

6 cups mixed bitter and/or wild greens (pages 10 and 11)
¾ cup hazelnuts (filberts), oven toasted (page 90)
3 tablespoons light olive oil or high-quality vegetable oil
3 tablespoons hazelnut oil or walnut oil
1 pound fresh wild mushrooms such as chanterelles, cèpes, morels, or shiitake, tough stems discarded and sliced about ¼ inch thick
2 tablespoons white wine vinegar or sherry vinegar
1 teaspoon Dijon-style mustard
Salt
6 ounces creamy blue cheese, crumbled
Freshly ground black pepper for serving

Grilled Vegetables and Goat Cheese Salad

Sun-Dried Tomato Vinaigrette
(page 82)
12 large radicchio leaves, blanched in
boiling water until pliable,
about 15 seconds
6 small rounds creamy mild goat's
milk cheese, about 2 inches in
diameter and 1 inch thick
Vegetable oil for brushing on grill
rack
2 or 3 medium-sized carrots, sliced on
the diagonal about ⅜ inch
thick, or 12 baby carrots, left
whole, boiled, steamed, or
microwaved until almost tender
6 small zucchini or other summer
squash, sliced about ⅜ inch
thick or left whole if very small
2 red sweet peppers, stems, seeds, and
membranes discarded, sliced
lengthwise about ⅜ inch thick
1 red onion, sliced crosswise about
⅜ inch thick
3 small leeks, including some green
tops, halved lengthwise
12 cherry tomatoes
Olive oil for brushing on cheese
bundles and vegetables
Fresh herb sprigs such as basil,
oregano, or summer savory for
garnish

Any seasonal vegetable may be substituted for those suggested; cook until done to preference. Fresh or canned grape leaves, kale, cabbage, or other greens may be used in place of the radicchio. For a heartier main dish, grill your favorite sausages, slice, and toss with the vegetables.

Prepare the vinaigrette and set aside.

Prepare a moderate to low fire in an open charcoal or gas grill for direct-heat cooking. Cover some cotton string for tying bundles with water and let soak for a few minutes.

Pat the blanched radicchio leaves dry with paper toweling. Wrap 2 leaves around each cheese round, overlapping them to prevent melting cheese from leaking out the seams. Tie the bundles with the dampened cotton string to hold the leaves in place.

When the fire is ready, lightly brush the grill rack with the vegetable oil and brush the cheese bundles and vegetables on all sides with the olive oil. Place the leaf-wrapped cheeses and the vegetables on the rack, positioning the vegetables over the hottest area of the fire for about 1 minute to sear. Turn the vegetables and sear the second sides for 1 minute. Move the vegetables to a cooler area and cook, turning frequently and brushing with olive oil as necessary, until just tender when pierced with a wooden skewer. Turn the cheese bundles after about 5 minutes and grill until the cheese is hot and feels slightly soft when pressed with the fingertips, about 3 minutes longer.

Transfer the vegetables to a large bowl and toss with the vinaigrette to taste.

Remove the string from the leaf-wrapped cheeses. Pull back the leaves on each bundle to expose part of the cheese. Arrange a cheese bundle and a portion of the vegetables on each individual plate. Garnish with the herb sprigs and serve warm.

Serves 6 as a salad course, or 3 as a main course.

Autumn Roots Salad

Herb Vinaigrette (page 81)
1 pound medium-sized beets
1 pound boiling potatoes or sweet potatoes, peeled and cut into ⅜-inch dice
1 pound large carrots, peeled and cut into ⅜-inch dice
1 pound celery root (celeriac), peeled and cut into ⅜-inch dice
1 pound turnips or rutabagas, peeled and cut into ⅜-inch dice
½ cup finely chopped green onion, including some green tops
½ cup minced fresh chervil or parsley, preferably flat-leaf type
Salt
Freshly ground black pepper
Fresh chervil or parsley springs or carrot greens for garnish

Serve this simple, earthy salad slightly warm or at room temperature; do not refrigerate. For a composed salad, keep each cooked vegetable separate, toss with some of the dressing and herbs, and arrange in individual mounds on each salad plate.

Prepare the vinaigrette and set aside.

Cut off leaves from the beets, leaving about a ½-inch stem. Place the beets in a saucepan, add water to cover, and bring to a boil over high heat. Cover the pot, reduce the heat to low, and simmer until just tender, about 30 minutes; older beets may take up to 1 hour. Alternatively, bake the beets in a preheated 350° F oven about 1 hour, or wrap each beet in plastic wrap and cook in a microwave oven at full power until tender when pierced, about 12 minutes. While still warm, peel the beets and cut into ⅜-inch dice. Transfer the beets to a bowl, toss with about one fourth of the vinaigrette, and set aside.

In four separate pans, cover the potatoes or sweet potatoes, carrots, celery root, and turnips or rutabagas with water and bring to a boil over high heat. Cover and cook until just tender when pierced, about 10 minutes for celery root, about 15 minutes for potatoes and carrots, and about 25 minutes for turnips or rutabagas. As each vegetable is done, drain and set aside. Alternatively, cook each vegetable in a microwave oven at full power until tender, about 7 minutes for celery root, about 5 minutes for potatoes and carrots, and 8 to 10 minutes for turnips or rutabagas.

Combine the potatoes, carrots, celery root, and turnips or rutabagas in a large bowl. Add the green onion, chervil or parsley, the remaining vinaigrette to taste, and salt and pepper to taste. Toss gently. Just before serving, gently stir the beets into the salad. Garnish with herb springs or carrot greens.

Serves 6 as a salad course, or 3 or 4 as a main course.

Spicy Black Bean and Corn Salad

Southwestern flavors meld in this robust composition, which I sometimes top with strips of grilled fish fillet or chicken breast or slices of pork tenderloin. For extra crunch, scatter Crunchy Tortilla Strips (page 92) over the top.

To prepare this salad ahead of time, combine the beans, corn, onions, chopped cilantro, and dressing, cover, and refrigerate for as long as overnight; bring to room temperature before adding the tomatoes, garnishing, and serving.

Prepare the vinaigrette and set aside.

Rinse the beans well under running cold water. Place in a saucepan, add water to cover, bring to a boil over high heat, and boil for 2 minutes. Remove from the heat and let stand, covered, for 1 hour. Drain.

Return beans to saucepan and add enough water to cover the beans by about 3 inches. Place over high heat and bring to a boil. Cover the saucepan with a lid slightly ajar, reduce the heat to low, and simmer for about 30 minutes. Stir in the cumin seed and 1 tablespoon salt and continue cooking until the beans are tender but still hold their shape, about 40 minutes longer. Drain well and cool.

In a large bowl, combine the beans, corn, red and green onions, cilantro, and the vinaigrette and toss well. Add the tomato and toss gently. Adjust the seasoning with salt. Garnish with cilantro sprigs and serve at room temperature.

Serves 8 as a salad course, or 4 as a main course.

Smoked Chile Vinaigrette (page 82)
2 cups (about 1 pound) black beans, picked over to remove grit or other foreign matter
1 tablespoon cumin seed
About 1 tablespoon salt
3 cups cooked fresh, drained canned, or thawed frozen corn kernels
½ cup minced red onion
½ cup minced green onion, including some green tops
½ cup chopped fresh cilantro (coriander)
2 cups chopped ripe tomato or halved cherry tomatoes
Fresh cilantro sprigs for garnish

Indonesian Vegetable Salad with Peanut Dressing (*Gado-Gado*)

Served throughout Indonesia and Malaysia, this salad offers an opportunity for great variety, as any assortment of seasonal vegetables may be used. Tradition dictates that the combination of vegetables may be cooked or raw, but never mixed. On this side of the Pacific, any mixture goes.

Suggestions for cooked vegetables include asparagus spears, small whole or sliced potatoes and carrots, broccoli and cauliflower florets, whole green beans and edible-podded peas, shelled fava beans, shredded Chinese cabbage, whole spinach leaves, and bean or sunflower sprouts.

Suitable raw vegetable additions include cucumber slices or sticks, tomato wedges or whole cherry tomatoes, red onion slices, short lengths of green onions, and strips of colorful sweet peppers.

Prepare the dressing and set aside.

If you wish to top the salad with fried shallot or onion slices, pour the oil into a deep-fat fryer or deep saucepan to a depth of about 2 inches. Heat to 365° F, or until a small cube of bread turns lightly golden within a few seconds of being dropped into the oil. Add the shallot or onion slices and deep-fry, stirring frequently, until golden brown. Using a slotted utensil, transfer the shallot or onion slices to paper toweling to drain.

Arrange the vegetables and eggs on a large platter. Sprinkle with the fried shallot or onion slices (if used) and garnish with the herb sprigs. Serve the dressing alongside.

Serves 6 as a salad course, or 3 or 4 as a main course.

Indonesian Peanut Dressing (page 88)
Peanut oil or other high-quality vegetable oil for deep-frying (optional)
2 cups thinly sliced shallot or yellow onion (optional)
About 6 cups assorted vegetables (see recipe introduction)
3 hard-cooked eggs, sliced or quartered
Fresh mint or cilantro (coriander) sprigs for garnish

Nut-Ball Salad

6 cups small whole mâche or curly
    spinach leaves or mixed salad
    greens (pages 10 and 11)
Avocado Dressing (page 85) or
    Tahini Dressing (page 86)
1 cup cashews
1 cup walnuts
1 cup sunflower seeds
1 cup coarsely chopped carrot
1 cup coarsely chopped red onion
1 cup coarsely chopped celery
About 2 tablespoons soy sauce,
    preferably tamari
2 eggs, lightly beaten
High-quality vegetable oil for
    deep-frying
About 12 cherry tomatoes, halved
    or quartered
Snipped fresh chives for sprinkling
Fresh rosemary or oregano sprigs for
    garnish

Lake Tahoe vegetarian friends Jan Ellis and Meri McEneny served me these little balls while I was working on this book. I thought they would be great in a salad.

The cashews and sunflower seeds may be raw, although roasted ones add more flavor.

Wash, dry, and chill the greens as described on page 10.

Prepare the dressing and set aside.

In a food processor, combine the nuts, seeds, carrot, onion, and celery and chop until fairly smooth. Alternatively, put the nuts, seeds, carrot, onion, and celery through a food grinder. Add the soy sauce to taste and the eggs. Form the mixture into balls about ¾ inch in diameter.

Pour the oil into a deep-fat fryer or a deep saucepan to a depth of 1 inch. Heat to 365° F, or until a small cube of bread turns lightly golden within a few seconds of being dropped into the oil. Drop the balls, a few at a time, into the oil and cook, turning frequently, until golden brown on all sides, about 8 minutes. Using a slotted utensil, transfer the balls to paper toweling to drain and cool.

Just before serving, spoon some of the dressing onto individual plates and top with the nut balls, greens, and tomatoes. Sprinkle with chives and garnish with herb sprigs.

Serves 6 to 8 as a salad course, or 3 or 4 as a main course.

Spaghetti Squash and Nut Salad

One 3- to 4-pound spaghetti squash
Citrus Vinaigrette (page 81), made
    with olive oil and equal portions
    of red wine vinegar and freshly
    squeezed orange or tangerine
    juice
½ cup hazelnuts (filberts), oven
    toasted (page 90)
½ cup pine nuts, pan toasted
    (page 91)
½ cup sunflower seeds, pan toasted
    (page 91)
2 large carrots, peeled
2 slender zucchini, about 5 inches
    long
Salt
⅔ cup chopped fresh chervil or
    parsley, preferably flat-leaf type
4 sun-dried tomatoes packed in olive
    oil, drained and cut into julienne
    strips
Zest of 1 orange or tangerine, cut
    into very thin julienne strips
Fresh chervil or parsley sprigs for
    garnish
Pesticide-free, nontoxic flowers such
    as violas or violets (optional)

Plenty of nuts and seeds add crunch to this simple salad.

Preheat an oven to 325° F.

With a long-tined fork or metal skewer, pierce the squash in several places to prevent the shell from bursting during cooking. Place the squash in a baking pan. Bake in the preheated oven until the shell gives a bit when pressed, or until the flesh is easily pierced with a fork, about 1½ to 2 hours. Alternatively, immerse the squash in a large pot of boiling water and cook until it is easily pierced, about 45 minutes.

Prepare the vinaigrette and set aside.

Toast the hazelnuts, coarsely chop, and set aside. Toast the pine nuts and sunflower seeds and set aside.

Using a vegetable peeler, slice the carrots and zucchini lengthwise into thin ribbons the entire length of the vegetable, then, with a sharp knife, cut each ribbon into strands to resemble spaghetti. Cook the carrot and zucchini strands separately in boiling, lightly salted water until tender-crisp. Drain, plunge into cold water to halt cooking, and drain again. Set aside.

When the spaghetti squash is cool enough to handle, cut the squash in half lengthwise and scoop out and discard the seeds and stringy portions. Using a fork, pull the pulp from the shell in long, thin strands and place them in a bowl. Season to taste with salt.

Add the carrot and zucchini strands, chopped chervil or parsley, tomatoes, and most of the citrus zest, and toasted hazelnuts, pine nuts, and sunflower seeds (save the rest for garnish). Add the vinaigrette to taste and toss well. Sprinkle with the remaining citrus zest, hazelnuts, pine nuts, and sunflower seeds. Garnish with the herb sprigs and flowers (if used).

Serves 6 to 8 as a salad course, or 4 as a light main course.

Toasted Bread Salad

About 5 cups mixed salad greens
(pages 10 and 11)
1 cup fresh small basil leaves or torn
larger leaves
About 8 ounces French or Italian
bread, sliced about 1 inch thick
2 large ripe tomatoes, chopped
3 tablespoons red wine vinegar or
white wine vinegar
⅓ cup fruity olive oil, preferably
extra-virgin
Salt
Freshly ground black pepper

The Italians prepare several different bread salads, including the very simple *panzanella,* in which stale bread is soaked in water, squeezed dry, tossed with tomatoes, red wine vinegar, olive oil, and chopped basil, and then allowed to stand for about an hour before serving. Another version, *pane a caponata,* combines toasted bread with tomatoes, assorted pickled vegetables, and fresh oregano and parsley, all tossed in fruity olive oil, of course.

For this bread salad, I use whole-grain levain bread from the Acme Bakery in Oakland, although any coarse-grained French or Italian loaf will work. My assistant Ellen prefers the salad with equal portions of vinegar and oil; if you enjoy tartness, add more vinegar.

Wash, dry, and chill the greens and basil leaves as described on page 10.

Preheat an oven to 300° F.

Cut the bread slices into 1-inch cubes and arrange them in a single layer on a baking sheet. Toast in the preheated oven, stirring frequently, until golden, about 15 minutes. Remove the bread cubes from the oven and let them cool to room temperature.

In a large salad bowl, combine the greens, basil, tomato, toasted bread, vinegar, and olive oil. Season with salt and pepper to taste and toss well.

Serves 6 to 8 as a salad course, or 3 or 4 as a light main course.

Asian Noodle Salad

Asian-Style Vinaigrette (page 81)
4 quarts water
About 1 tablespoon salt
1 pound fresh or dried thin Asian
    wheat noodles or dried thin
    Italian noodles such as
    spaghettini
8 ounces snow peas, cut on the
    diagonal into rectangles
1 cup finely chopped green onion,
    including some green tops
1 cup coarsely chopped unsalted
    dry-roasted peanuts
½ cup chopped fresh cilantro
    (coriander)

For a more substantial dish, add bite-sized pieces of poached chicken breast, roast duck, cooked shrimp, or other poultry or seafood. Double the recipe for the vinaigrette and be generous with the chile oil.

If you wish to make the salad a day before serving, omit the snow peas when tossing. Cover and refrigerate; bring to room temperature before adding the snow peas and serving.

Prepare the vinaigrette and set aside.

In a large pot, bring the water to a rapid boil over high heat. Add the salt, drop in the noodles, and stir vigorously. Cook, stirring frequently, until barely tender and still quite firm to the bite, about 1 minute for fresh noodles or 5 to 8 minutes for dried noodles; do not cook quite as much as for a hot noodle dish. Drain, rinse quickly under running cold water, and drain again. Transfer the noodles to a large bowl, add about half of the vinaigrette, and toss well. Cool to room temperature, stirring occasionally to keep noodle strands from sticking together.

Bring a large saucepan filled with water to a boil. Add the snow peas and cook until tender-crisp, about 1 minute. Drain, then plunge into ice water to halt cooking and preserve color. Drain well.

Add the snow peas, green onion, peanuts, cilantro, and the remaining vinaigrette to the noodles and toss gently but thoroughly. Serve at room temperature.

Serves 8 to 10 as a salad course, or 4 or 5 as a light main course.

Mixed Grain and Herb Tabbouleh

¼ cup bulgur (cracked wheat)
2½ cups boiling water
2½ teaspoons plus ¼ cup fruity olive
    oil, preferably extra-virgin
½ cup brown rice
1 cup cold water
½ cup millet
¾ cup minced fresh parsley,
    preferably flat-leaf type
¾ cup minced mixed fresh herbs such
    as basil, chervil, mint, oregano,
    sage, and summer savory
½ cup minced green onion, including
    some green tops
1 cup chopped ripe tomato, peeled
    and seeded if desired
¼ cup freshly squeezed lemon juice,
    or to taste
About 1 teaspoon salt
About 1 tablespoon freshly ground
    black pepper
Fresh herb sprigs (same as used in
    salad) for garnish

Middle Eastern tabbouleh is usually made with bulgur and fresh parsley. Here is a change-of-pace version made with several grains and a bouquet of fresh herbs. For a quick-and-easy variation, increase the bulgur to 1 cup and omit the rice and millet. In any case, be sure to use only fresh herbs, never dried.

In a large bowl, cover the bulgur with 1½ cups of the boiling water and let stand for 2 hours. Drain well.

Meanwhile, heat 1 teaspoon of the oil in a small, heavy saucepan over medium heat. Add the rice and stir to coat well. Add the 1 cup cold water and bring to a boil. Stir once, cover, reduce the heat to low, and cook for 45 minutes. Remove from the heat and let stand for 10 minutes. Fluff with a fork and transfer to a large bowl to cool to room temperature.

To cook the millet, heat 1 teaspoon of the oil in a small, heavy saucepan over medium heat. Add the millet and cook until lightly browned and nutty smelling, stirring or shaking the pan continuously, about 3 minutes. Add the remaining 1 cup boiling water and ½ teaspoon of the remaining oil and stir once. Cover, reduce the heat to very low, and cook until done, about 25 minutes. Remove from the heat, remove the lid, cover the top of the pot with paper toweling, replace the lid, and let stand for 10 minutes. Fluff with a fork and transfer to a bowl to cool to room temperature.

In a large bowl, combine the drained bulgur, cooled rice and millet, herbs, onion, tomato, lemon juice, and the remaining ¼ cup oil. Season with salt and pepper to taste. Garnish with herb sprigs.

Serves 6 as a salad course.

Seafood Salad

About 30 tender lettuce leaves
Creamy Fresh Herb Dressing
    (page 84)
1 pound medium-sized shrimp in the
    shell, boiled until tender,
    drained, and chilled, then peeled
    with tails left intact
1 pound cooked fresh crab meat
1 pound cooked fresh lobster meat
1 pound small mussels, well scrubbed,
    beards removed, steamed until
    shells open, and chilled
16 small oysters on the half shell
6 hard-cooked eggs, halved or
    quartered, for garnish
Fresh caviar (one type or a
    combination) for garnish
Lemon wedges for serving

Combine whatever seafood is freshest in your area.

Wash, dry, and chill the whole lettuce leaves as described on page 10.

Prepare the dressing and set aside.

Just before serving, line a serving platter or individual plates with the lettuce leaves. Arrange the seafood on top. Serve the dressing alongside. Garnish with the eggs and caviar. Offer the lemon wedges for squeezing over the top at the table.

Serves 8 as a salad course, or 4 as a main course.

Lobster and Spicy Cabbage Salad

This sublime combination is based on a salad served by Matt Adams, chef/owner of Christy Hill on the north shore of Lake Tahoe, one of my favorite restaurants anywhere.

Combine the water, celery, onion, and parsley in a large pot and bring to a boil over high heat. Drop the lobsters head first into the boiling water and cook until the shells turn bright red and the meat is opaque, about 8 minutes. Remove the lobsters, drain, and set aside until cool enough to handle.

Break the lobster tail off each body. Using scissors, cut a lengthwise slit along the soft underpart of the tail; remove the meat and discard the vein that runs along the back. Split each tail in half lengthwise and set aside. Crack the claws, carefully remove the meat, and set aside. The lobster meat can be covered and refrigerated for as long as overnight; return it to room temperature before serving.

Prepare the dressing. Pour about two thirds of it over the cabbage and toss well. Let stand for about 15 minutes.

To serve as a salad course, mound about one fourth of the cabbage on each of 4 individual plates. Arrange half a tail and the meat from 1 claw on each plate. To serve as a main course, arrange 1 split tail and the meat from 2 claws on each dinner plate. Drizzle lobster meat with the remaining dressing and sprinkle with the green onions and cilantro. Garnish with sweet pepper. Offer the lime or lemon wedges for squeezing over the top at the table.

Serves 4 as a salad course, or 2 as a light main course.

2 gallons water
2 celery stalks, chopped
1 yellow onion, quartered
3 or 4 fresh parsley sprigs
2 live Maine lobsters (about 1 pound each)
Thai-Style Dressing (page 87)
3 cups shredded cabbage, preferably Asian type such as Napa
2 green onions, including some green tops, thinly sliced
¼ cup minced fresh cilantro (coriander) for garnish
Julienned red sweet pepper, placed in iced water until curled, for garnish
Lime or lemon wedges for serving

Southeast Asian Warm Spicy Shrimp Salad

Tangy dressing adorns cool greens and warm shrimp for a tantalizing juxtaposition.

Wash, dry, and chill the greens as described on page 10.

In a medium-sized bowl, combine the shrimp, garlic, minced chile or chile sauce, fish sauce or soy sauce, sugar, and white pepper to taste. Cover and let stand at room temperature for about 30 minutes, stirring several times.

Prepare the dressing and set aside.

Just before serving, heat a wok or deep skillet over high heat. Add the oil and swirl to coat the pan. When the oil is hot, add the shrimp and stir-fry until the shrimp turn bright pink and the meat is opaque, about 2 minutes. Remove from the heat.

In a salad bowl, toss the greens with some of the dressing to taste. Distribute among individual plates and top with the warm shrimp. Drizzle some of the remaining dressing over the shrimp and serve immediately.

Serves 6 as a salad course, or 3 or 4 as a main course.

About 6 cups mixed salad greens (pages 10 and 11)
1½ pounds medium-sized shrimp in the shell, peeled with tails left intact
2 tablespoons minced or pressed garlic
1 tablespoon minced fresh red hot chile, or 1 tablespoon Asian chile sauce or Tabasco sauce
2 tablespoons fish sauce, or 1 tablespoon soy sauce
1 teaspoon sugar
About 1 tablespoon freshly ground white pepper
Southeast Asian Lime Dressing (page 88)
3 tablespoons peanut oil or other high-quality vegetable oil

Crab and Melon with Mint Vinaigrette

Herb Vinaigrette (page 81), made
    with lemon juice and fresh mint
About 6 pounds assorted ripe melons
    such as yellow and red
    watermelon, orange and green
    honeydew, Crenshaw, or
    Canary
1 pound cooked fresh crab meat
Fresh mint sprigs for garnish
Nasturtiums or other pesticide-free,
    nontoxic flowers for garnish
Cooked king crab legs for garnish
    (optional)

A delightfully cooling combination for a summer day.

Prepare the vinaigrette and set aside.

Cut the melons in half, remove the seeds, and cut the pulp into geometric shapes; you'll need about 6 cups. Place the cut-up melon in a large bowl. Save any remaining melon for another purpose.

Toss the melon with about one third of the vinaigrette and set aside.

Place the crab in a small bowl, add about one half of the remaining vinaigrette and toss; set aside.

To serve, arrange the melon on individual plates or on a serving platter. Top with the crab meat, drizzle with the remaining vinaigrette, and garnish with the mint sprigs, flowers, and crab legs (if used).

Serves 6 as a salad course, or 3 or 4 as a main course.

Curried Tuna Salad

½ cup plain yogurt
½ cup Mayonnaise (page 85) or high-
    quality commercial mayonnaise
1 tablespoon freshly squeezed lemon
    juice
2 tablespoons high-quality hot or
    mild curry powder, or to taste
¼ cup cashews or macadamia nuts,
    oven toasted (page 90)
1 pound fresh tuna fillets, grilled or
    poached, cooled, and flaked, or
    2 cans (7 ounces *each)* tuna
    packed in water, drained and
    flaked
1 cup finely chopped unpeeled apple
¼ cup finely chopped sweet pickle or
    pickle relish
½ cup raisins or dried currants,
    plumped in hot water for 15
    minutes and drained
2 tablespoons minced green onion,
    including some green tops
Minced fresh parsley, preferably
    flat-leaf type, for garnish

This quick-and-easy dish is a popular standby around my house. Even guests who claim not to like tuna salad have been known to change their minds once they taste this exceptional rendition. Although freshly poached, broiled, or grilled tuna creates a more flavorful version, canned tuna works just fine.

I sometimes serve the tuna mixture with whale lettuce leaves alongside for wrapping around a scoop of the salad as a breadless sandwich.

In a small bowl, combine the yogurt, Mayonnaise, lemon juice, and curry powder. Blend well and set aside.

Toast the nuts, chop coarsely, and set aside.

In a larger bowl, combine the tuna, apple, pickle or pickle relish, drained raisins or currants, onion, and toasted nuts. Stir in the yogurt dressing to taste. Transfer to a serving bowl or mound on a platter or individual plates and sprinkle with parsley.

Serves 4 as a salad course, or 2 as a main course.

Mediterranean Roast Chicken and Vegetable Salad

One 3½- to 4-pound chicken
About ⅓ cup fruity olive oil,
    preferably extra-virgin
⅓ cup minced equal parts fresh basil,
    lavender, rosemary, summer
    savory, and thyme, or 2
    tablespoons crumbled dried
    herbes de Provence
Salt
Freshly ground black pepper
1 pound new potatoes
1 pound eggplant, cut into 1-inch
    cubes
1 large red or yellow onion, cut into
    wedges
2 red sweet peppers, stems, seeds, and
    membranes discarded, cut into
    1-inch squares
1 head garlic, separated into cloves
    and peeled
6 ounces drained marinated artichoke
    hearts, thinly sliced
½ cup slivered, pitted oil-cured ripe
    olives
Mustard Vinaigrette (page 81), made
    with Dijon-style mustard
8 ounces green beans, trimmed, cut
    into 3-inch lengths and cooked
    until tender-crisp
1 cup chopped fresh basil
½ cup chopped fresh parsley,
    preferably flat-leaf type
8 ounces feta cheese, cut into
    ½-inch cubes
Fresh basil or parsley sprigs for
    garnish

Redolent of garlic and the herbs typical of Mediterranean gardens, this robust salad is a simple one-dish meal.

Preheat an oven to 375° F.

Quickly rinse the chicken under running cold water and pat dry with paper toweling. Rub the chicken all over with a little of the olive oil, then sprinkle lightly with some of the herbs and salt and pepper to taste. Place the chicken on a rack in a roasting pan. Roast, uncovered, in the preheated oven for 10 minutes. Reduce the heat to 350° F and roast, basting with any pan drippings every 15 minutes if desired, until golden brown and the juices run clear when the thickest part of the thigh is pierced, 1 hour to 1 hour and 20 minutes. Remove the chicken from the oven and cool to room temperature, then cut or shred the meat into bite-sized pieces and place in a large bowl.

Meanwhile, prepare the vegetables. If the potatoes are small, leave them whole; if they are large, cut them into halves or quarters. Combine the potatoes, eggplant, onion, sweet peppers, garlic, the remaining minced or crumbled herbs, and salt and pepper to taste in a shallow roasting pan. Toss together with just enough of the remaining olive oil to coat the vegetables. Roast in the oven with the chicken, stirring occasionally, until the vegetables are tender but still hold their shape when pierced with a wooden skewer or fork, about 30 minutes. Transfer to the bowl with the chicken. Add the artichoke hearts and olives.

Prepare the vinaigrette and pour about half of it over the chicken and vegetables. Let stand at room temperature for at least 15 minutes, or for up to 30 minutes. Or cool to room temperature, cover, and chill for as long as overnight; return to room temperature before serving.

Just before serving, add the green beans, chopped basil and parsley, and cheese and toss thoroughly, adding the remaining dressing to taste. Garnish with fresh herb sprigs.

Serves 10 to 12 as a salad course, or 6 as a main course.

Japanese Rice and Chicken Salad

1 pound fresh spinach leaves
Creamy Japanese Dressing (page 87)
2 cups long-grain white rice,
    thoroughly rinsed and drained
3 cups homemade chicken stock,
    canned chicken broth, or water
4 boned and skinned chicken breast
    halves
Sesame seeds, preferably black
    variety, pan toasted, (page 91),
    for garnish
1 cup diced carrot, steamed or boiled
    until tender-crisp, then rinsed
    in cold water to halt cooking
    and drained
8 ounces whole *enokitake* (slender
    Japanese white mushrooms),
    stem ends trimmed, or oyster
    mushrooms or common white
    mushrooms, tough stems
    discarded, sliced and steamed
    until just tender if desired
6 green onions, including some green
    tops, thinly sliced on the
    diagonal
Julienned red sweet pepper for
    garnish

Serve this room-temperature salad, which combines the flavors of classic *mizutaki,* as a main course on a hot day. Although most Japanese prefer slightly sticky short-grain rice, fluffier long-grain rice is better for a salad.

Wash, dry, and chill the spinach as described on page 10.

Prepare the dressing, cover, and refrigerate for at least 1 hour or as long as overnight; return almost to room temperature before using.

In a heavy saucepan, combine the drained rice and the stock, broth, or water. Bring to a boil over high heat, then stir once, reduce the heat to very low, cover tightly, and simmer for 17 minutes. (Follow package directions for cooking parboiled or converted rice.) Do not remove the cover or stir during cooking. Remove the saucepan from the heat and fluff the rice with a fork. Transfer the rice to a large mixing bowl and let cool slightly. Gently toss the warm rice with about one third of the dressing. Fluff frequently until the rice cools to room temperature.

Meanwhile, place the chicken breasts in a large saucepan in which they fit comfortably. Add just enough cold water to cover the breasts. Bring the water to a boil, then immediately reduce the heat so that the water barely ripples. Simmer until the meat is opaque throughout, just beyond the pink stage, about 12 minutes. Using a slotted utensil, remove the breasts to a plate. Let cool to room temperature, then cut into bite-sized pieces.

Toast the sesame seeds and set aside.

Add the chicken, carrot, mushrooms, and about half of the green onions to the cooled rice and toss. Add the remaining dressing to taste and toss to coat well.

Arrange the spinach on a large platter or on individual plates, or line a large bowl or individual bowls with the spinach leaves. Top with the rice mixture, sprinkle with the toasted sesame seeds and the remaining green onions, and garnish with the sweet pepper strips.

Serves 6 to 8 as a salad course, or 4 as a main course.

Southern Fried Salad

It seems that every innovative restaurant chef from Paul Prudhomme in New Orleans to Bradley Ogden in Larkspur, California, prepares a fried chicken salad. The counterpoint achieved between warm fried chicken and cool, crisp greens is so good that I had to create my own version of this new dish destined to become an American classic.

For a seafood version, substitute catfish filets or oysters for the chicken, and use finely ground cornmeal instead of the flour in the coating mix.

Wash, dry, and chill the greens as described on page 10.

Quickly rinse the chicken under running cold water and pat dry with paper toweling. Cut the chicken into finger-thick strips or bite-sized chunks. Place in a bowl and add the milk or buttermilk to cover. Refrigerate, covered, for 1 to 3 hours. Return to room temperature before cooking.

Prepare the dressing or vinaigrette and set aside.

In a shallow bowl, combine all the ingredients for the coating mix and stir to blend thoroughly. Set aside.

Pour the oil into a deep-fat fryer or deep saucepan to a depth of about 2 inches. Heat to 375° F, or until a small cube of bread turns lightly golden within a few seconds of being dropped into the oil.

Dredge the chicken pieces in the coating mix, turning to coat all sides. Add a few of the chicken pieces to the oil and cook, turning occasionally, until crisp and brown, about 8 minutes. Using a slotted utensil, transfer the chicken to paper toweling to drain. Keep warm in a 200° F oven. Repeat with the remaining chicken.

Just before serving, toss the greens in about half of the dressing or vinaigrette. Arrange the greens on individual plates and top with the fried chicken, cheese, and beets or pickles. Drizzle with the remaining dressing or vinaigrette, sprinkle with the bacon bits, and serve immediately.

Serves 6 to 8 as a salad course, or 3 or 4 as a main course.

About 6 cups curly chicory, dandelion greens or mixed salad greens (pages 10 and 11)
6 boned and skinned chicken breast halves
About 3 cups milk or buttermilk
Honey Dressing (page 89) or Mustard Vinaigrette (page 81)

SPICY COATING
1½ cups all-purpose flour
1 tablespoon minced or pressed garlic, or 1 tablespoon garlic powder
1 tablespoon freshly ground black pepper
1 tablespoon freshly ground white pepper
1 tablespoon ground dried red chile pepper
2 tablespoons minced fresh thyme, or 2 teaspoons crumbled dried thyme
About 1 teaspoon salt

High-quality vegetable oil for deep-frying
About 12 ounces creamy blue cheese, broken into chunks
1 cup small whole or sliced pickled beets or sliced bread-and-butter pickles
Crispy Bacon Bits (page 91), preferably made with pepper bacon or pancetta

Green Papaya Chicken Salad

Southeast Asian Lime Dressing
(page 88)
2 boned and skinned chicken breast
halves
1½ pounds green papayas
4 ounces snow peas or green beans
1 medium-sized carrot, peeled
½ cup coarsely chopped fresh mint
½ cup coarsely chopped fresh
cilantro (coriander)
¼ cup minced green onion, including
some green tops
⅓ cup coarsely chopped unsalted
dry-roasted peanuts
Fresh mint and/or cilantro sprigs for
garnish

Variations on this salad, usually eaten as a snack, are found throughout Southeast Asia. In the dish, firm green papayas take on the role of a crisp vegetable. When you can't find green, or unripe, papayas in markets that sell Southeast Asian or Caribbean foods, substitute unripe mangoes, or use jicama, tart apples, parsnips, turnips, or cabbage.

Ground dried shrimp is more authentic than the chicken used here. The result will still be delicious if you substitute cooked shrimp, shredded grilled beef, or other meats.

Prepare the dressing and set aside.

Place the chicken breasts in a saucepan in which they fit comfortably. Add just enough cold water to cover the breasts. Bring the water to a boil, then immediately reduce the heat so that the water barely ripples. Simmer until the meat is opaque throughout, just beyond the pink stage, about 12 minutes. Using a slotted utensil, transfer the breasts to a plate. Let cool to room temperature, then shred or slice into long julienne strips.

Peel and seed the papayas and cut the flesh into long julienne strips. Cut the snow peas or beans and carrot into the same width julienne strips. Briefly blanch the snowpeas or beans and carrot in boiling water and quickly plunge in cold water to halt cooking and preserve color.

In a large bowl, combine the papaya, snow peas or beans, and carrot. Add the shredded chicken, chopped mint and cilantro, green onion, about half of the peanuts, and about three fourths of the dressing. Using your hands, toss the mixture thoroughly while squeezing lightly to release the flavors. Taste and add more dressing, if needed. Transfer the salad to a serving platter or bowl, sprinkle with the remaining peanuts, and garnish with the fresh herb sprigs.

Serves 6 as a salad course or snack, or 3 or 4 as a main course.

Smoked Turkey and Wild Rice Salad

Smoked turkey is readily available in delicatessens and specialty-food markets. Alternatively, smoke your own turkey, following the directions supplied with your smoker.

Prepare the salad and refrigerate at least several hours before serving, or preferably overnight, to allow flavors to meld. Return the salad to room temperature before serving.

Prepare the nuts and set aside.

Prepare the dressing and set aside.

To cook the rice, place it in a wire strainer and wash thoroughly under running cold water until the water runs clear. Drain. In a heavy saucepan over high heat, bring the stock or broth to a boil. Add the rice and return to a boil. Stir once, cover, reduce the heat to low, and simmer until the rice is just tender, about 35 to 40 minutes. Remove from the heat and drain off any excess water. Cover the pot with a piece of paper toweling, replace the lid, and let stand until the rice is dry, about 5 minutes. Fluff the rice with a fork, lifting from the bottom instead of stirring. Transfer the rice to a large bowl and let cool to room temperature, stirring occasionally.

Add the turkey, green and red onions, red pepper, parsley, and salt and pepper to taste. Add about three fourths of the dressing and toss thoroughly. Add more dressing, if needed. Serve the salad surrounded with the papaya (if used). Sprinkle with the nuts just before serving.

Serves 8 as a salad course, or 4 as a main course.

Sweet Crunchy Nuts (page 90), made with walnut or pecan halves
Papaya-Seed Dressing (page 89)
2 cups wild rice
1 quart homemade turkey or chicken stock or canned chicken broth
3 cups cubed smoked turkey breast
3 green onions, including some green tops, thinly sliced
½ cup minced red onion
1 cup minced red sweet pepper
½ cup minced fresh parsley, preferably flat-leaf type
Salt
Freshly ground black pepper
Diced ripe papaya (optional)

California Chinese Duck Salad

If time is limited, use a roasted duck or chicken from a delicatessen or a roasted duck from a Chinese market for the duck breasts. Make cracklings from the skin of these birds and shred or slice the meat.

Wash, dry, and chill the lettuce or cabbage as described on page 10.

Toast the sesame seeds and set aside.

In a large bowl, combine the soy sauce, ginger, garlic, and 2 tablespoons of the hoisin sauce. Add the duck breasts and turn to coat on all sides. Let stand at room temperature for about 15 minutes.

Heat a sauté pan or skillet over medium-high heat. Add the duck breasts, skin side down, and cook until the skin is browned, about 7 minutes. Pour off the fat. Turn the breasts and cook until the second sides are lightly browned, 2 to 3 minutes. Remove from the heat and let cool slightly. Remove the skin and bones from the meat. Pull or slice the meat into long, thin shreds and set aside. Slice the skin into long, thin strips. Heat a skillet over high heat, add the skin, and sauté until crisp and golden brown, about 10 minutes. Using a slotted utensil, remove the cracklings to paper toweling to drain.

In a bowl, combine the duck meat with the remaining 2 tablespoons hoisin sauce, the sesame oil, tomatoes, and about half of the green onion, peanuts, and toasted sesame seeds. Add chile oil to taste. Set aside.

Pour the oil into a wok or deep skillet to a depth of about ½ inch. Heat to about 360° F, or until a rice stick puffs up within seconds of being dropped into the oil. Add a small handful of the rice sticks and cook, turning once, until puffed, crisp, and lightly golden, 12 to 15 seconds. Using a slotted utensil, transfer the noodles to paper toweling to drain. Repeat with the remaining rice sticks.

Spread the lettuce or cabbage on a serving platter or individual plates and top with about half of the fried rice sticks and half of the duck mixture. Add the remaining rice sticks and duck. Scatter the mango and duck cracklings over the top. Sprinkle with the remaining green onion, sesame seeds, and peanuts and garnish with the cilantro.

Serves 8 as a salad course, or 4 as a main course.

1 head crisp lettuce such as romaine or Asian-type cabbage, shredded
¼ cup sesame seeds, pan toasted (page 91)
2 tablespoons soy sauce
1 tablespoon minced fresh ginger root
1 teaspoon minced or pressed garlic
¼ cup hoisin sauce
4 duck breast halves with skin intact, trimmed of excess fat
2 tablespoons Asian-style sesame oil
4 sun-dried tomatoes in olive oil, drained and cut in julienne strips
½ cup minced green onion, including some green tops
¼ cup finely chopped unsalted dry-roasted peanuts
About 2 teaspoons hot chile oil
Peanut oil or other high-quality vegetable oil for deep-frying
4 ounces dried rice sticks (wiry rice-flour noodles), broken into small bunches
1 ripe mango, peeled, seeded, and cut into small dice
Fresh cilantro (coriander) sprigs or leaves for garnish

Cobb Salad, Southwestern Style

1 head crisp lettuce such as romaine
    or iceberg
1 teaspoon minced or pressed garlic
1 tablespoon ground dried red chile
    pepper, preferably ancho or
    pasilla
2 tablespoons minced fresh oregano,
    or 1 tablespoon crumbled dried
    oregano
About 1 teaspoon salt
1 pound boneless lean pork, trimmed
    of excess fat, sliced about
    ½ inch thick, or 2 boned and
    skinned chicken breast halves
Basic Vinaigrette (page 80)
2 cups pine nuts, pan toasted
    (page 91)
2 cups chopped, peeled ripe tomato
2 cups cooked fresh, drained canned,
    or thawed frozen corn kernels
2 cups chopped, cooked fresh prickly
    pear cactus pad (nopal) or
    drained canned cactus pad
2 cups (about 8 ounces) goat's milk
    cheese, crumbled
Fresh oregano or cilantro (coriander)
    sprigs or pesticide-free edible
    flowers such as calendula
    (pot marigold) for garnish

This old standard, invented at Hollywood's Brown Derby restaurant during the film capital's heyday, is unique: a bed of finely chopped lettuce topped with bands of other uniformly cut ingredients is tossed together at the table. Traditional components include crisply fried bacon, cooked chicken breast, hard-cooked egg, blue cheese, and ripe avocado and tomato. Although the original combo is hard to beat, here is a variation that uses popular southwestern ingredients.

Adapt the idea to other ethnic cuisines. An Italian Cobb, for example, might be topped with cooked pancetta, sun-dried tomatoes, Gorgonzola, toasted pine nuts, artichoke hearts, and fresh basil.

Wash, dry, and chill the whole lettuce leaves as described on page 10.

Prepare a hot fire in an open charcoal or gas grill for direct-heat cooking, or preheat a broiler.

In a small bowl, combine the garlic, ground pepper, minced or crumbled oregano, and salt to taste and rub the mixture all over the pork or chicken. Let stand about 20 minutes.

Prepare the vinaigrette and set aside.

Toast the pine nuts and set aside.

Grill or broil the meat, turning once, just until done, 4 to 6 minutes per side. When cool enough to handle, cut the meat into pieces about the size of corn kernels.

Just before serving, finely chop the lettuce and spread it evenly on a serving platter or place it in a salad bowl. Arrange the cooked meat, pine nuts, tomato, corn, cactus, and cheese on top. Garnish with the herb sprigs or flowers.

At the table, pour about three fourths of the dressing over the salad and toss well. Add more dressing if needed and serve immediately.

Serves 6 to 8 as a salad course, or 4 as a main course.

Grilled Pancetta-Wrapped Figs and Arugula with Lavender Dressing

½ cup fruity olive oil, preferably
    extra-virgin
1 tablespoon chopped fresh lavender
    flowers, or 1½ teaspoons
    crumbled dried lavender flowers
About 6 cups arugula or
    other assertive greens
    (pages 10 and 11)
½ cup pine nuts, pan toasted (page 91)
16 large fresh black figs
16 thin slices pancetta or smoked
    pepper bacon (about 1 pound)
Vegetable oil for brushing grill
About 4 teaspoons balsamic vinegar
    or red wine vinegar
Fresh lavender blossoms for garnish
    (optional)
Lemon wedges for serving

Whenever figs are in season, I incorporate them into my meals in as many different ways as possible. If you don't have pancetta (Italian-style bacon) or pepper-cured bacon, substitute regular bacon and liberally sprinkle the cooked figs with freshly ground black pepper. When you don't want to fire up a grill, cook the bacon-wrapped fruits under a broiler.

The oil for the dressing should be prepared at least a day, preferably longer, in advance of making the salad. If you wish, use the oil to make Mustard Vinaigrette (page 81) for tossing the greens instead of the simple coating suggested.

In a bowl or jar, combine the olive oil and chopped or crumbled lavender, cover, and let stand at room temperature for at least 24 hours or for up to several weeks. Strain before using.

Wash, dry, and chill the arugula or other greens as described on page 10.

Toast the pine nuts and set aside.

Prepare a moderate fire in an open charcoal or gas grill for direct-heat cooking.

Wrap each fig with a piece of bacon and secure the bacon in place with a toothpick or small metal skewer. Brush the grill rack with vegetable oil. Place figs on the rack and grill, turning frequently, until the bacon is browned, about 5 minutes.

In a bowl, drizzle the arugula or other greens with oil and toss to coat lightly. Sprinkle with vinegar and toss again. Divide the greens among 4 individual salad plates or 2 dinner plates. Arrange the figs on each plate and drizzle with a little more of the lavender oil and vinegar. Sprinkle with the pine nuts and garnish with lavender blossoms (if used). Offer the lemon wedges for squeezing over the top at the table.

Serves 4 as a salad course, or 2 as a main course.

Potato-Leek Salad with Spicy Sausage Dressing

For a vegetarian version, prepare Mustard Vinaigrette (page 81) instead of the Spicy Sausage Dressing and sprinkle with Mimosa Topping (page 93).

1½ pounds boiling potatoes
Spicy Sausage Dressing (page 83)
Salt
Freshly ground black pepper
12 small to medium-sized leeks
1 cup chopped ripe tomato, peeled
    and seeded if desired
About ¼ cup coarsely chopped fresh
    parsley, preferably flat-leaf
    type, or tarragon

Wash the potatoes under running cold water, scrubbing well to remove all traces of soil. Place them in a saucepan, add cold water to cover by about 2 inches, and remove the potatoes. Bring the water to a boil over medium-high heat, add the potatoes, and cook until tender when pierced with a wooden skewer or small, sharp knife, about 10 minutes for small potatoes or 15 to 20 minutes for larger ones. Drain, return the potatoes to the pan, and set over the heat. Shake the pan until the moisture evaporates and the potatoes are dry to the touch.

Meanwhile, prepare the dressing and set aside.

Peel the potatoes, if desired, cut them into ¼-inch-thick slices, and place in a bowl. Season to taste with salt and pepper. Cool slightly, then add just enough of the dressing to coat lightly and toss gently to mix thoroughly.

Cut off and discard the root ends and the tough dark green tops from the leeks. Strip away and discard any tough outer layers. Cut the leeks in half lengthwise and rinse under running cold water, exposing the layers with your fingers so that all the grit washes away. Leave the leek halves whole or cut them into 3- to 4-inch lengths. Arrange the leeks in a single layer in a large shallow pan. Add water to cover barely and place over medium-high heat. Bring to a boil and cook, uncovered, until tender when pierced with a wooden skewer, about 12 minutes. Remove from the heat and drain well. Season to taste with salt and pepper. Pour the remaining dressing over the leeks and let stand about 15 minutes.

Remove the leeks from the dressing and arrange them with the potatoes in alternating stripes on a serving platter or individual plates. Sprinkle with the tomato and chopped herb and drizzle with the dressing remaining in the leek pan. Serve at room temperature.

Serves 6 as a salad course, or 3 or 4 as a light main course.

Warm White Bean Salad with Bresaola

Italian *bresaola*, air-dried beef fillet, has a more delicate flavor than prosciutto, its better-known pork counterpart. Although the Italian product is not permitted through United States customs, good versions made in California or imported from Switzerland are becoming more readily available. Prosciutto or cured American-style ham such as Smithfield or Virginia may be substituted for the beef.

Rinse the beans well under running cold water. Place in a bowl, add cold water to cover, and let stand overnight to soak.

Wash, dry, and chill the greens as described on page 10.

Drain the beans and transfer to a saucepan. Add the sage, garlic, salt and pepper to taste, and enough cold water to cover the beans by about 3 inches. Place over high heat and bring to a boil. Cover the saucepan with a lid slightly ajar, reduce the heat to low, and simmer until the beans are tender but still hold their shape, about 45 minutes to 1 hour. If using the beans immediately, drain well and transfer to a bowl. Taste and add more salt and pepper if desired. If cooked ahead, cool the undrained beans, cover, and refrigerate; reheat and drain shortly before serving.

Add the vinegar and oil to the warm beans and toss well. Arrange the beans on a platter or individual plates. Top with the *bresaola*, greens, and cheese and serve immediately.

Serves 6 as a salad course, or 3 as a main course.

2 cups dried cannellini or Great Northern beans
About 4 cups arugula, mizuna, or other bitter or assertive greens (pages 10 and 11)
½ cup whole fresh sage leaves, or ¼ cup dried sage leaves
2 garlic cloves
About ½ teaspoon salt
Freshly ground black pepper
3 tablespoons white wine vinegar
½ cup fruity olive oil, preferably extra-virgin
14 ounces *bresaola*, thinly sliced
About 1 cup freshly shaved Parmesan cheese, preferably parmigiano-reggiano

Smoked Veal Loin with Tomato Chutney and Horseradish

This salad is my interpretation of a similar feast I enjoyed several times one summer at Wolfdale's, an imaginative restaurant on the north shore of Lake Tahoe. You may substitute smoked, grilled, or roasted pork or beef tenderloin or poultry for the veal.

Prepare the chutney and set aside.

In a food processor or a blender, combine the soy sauce, wine or beer, oil, vinegar, onion, ginger, garlic, sugar, and mustard. Blend thoroughly. Place the veal loin in a shallow dish and pour the soy sauce mixture over it. Cover and refrigerate overnight, turning the meat several times. Return to room temperature before cooking.

Following instructions in your smoker manufacturer's manual, prepare a fire with charcoal and presoaked aromatic hardwood chips. Position the smoker pan under the grill.

Remove the veal loin from the marinade and pour the marinade into the smoker pan. Brush the smoker rack with oil and position the veal on it over the liquid. Smoke slowly until the meat is rare, about 6 hours, adding more coals and presoaked chips as needed to maintain the fire. If you desire the meat more thoroughly cooked, roast or grill it to your preference after smoking.

Wash, dry, and chill the greens as described on page 10.

Prepare the vinaigrette and set aside.

Remove the meat from the smoker and let cool to room temperature. Cut the veal into ½-inch-thick slices.

To serve, toss the greens with the vinaigrette to taste and arrange them on individual plates. Arrange 2 or 3 slices smoked veal, dollops of chutney and horseradish, olives, and cheese on each plate.

Serves 8 as a salad course, or 6 as a main course.

Tomato Chutney (page 93)
¾ cup soy sauce
1 cup dry white wine or flat beer
3 tablespoons high-quality vegetable oil
2 tablespoons rice vinegar or white wine vinegar
3 tablespoons coarsely chopped yellow onion
3 tablespoons coarsely chopped fresh ginger root
2 or 3 whole garlic cloves
1 tablespoon sugar
1 teaspoon dry mustard
One 3- to 4-pound boneless veal loin, trimmed of excess fat
Vegetable oil for brushing on smoker rack
About 6 cups mixed salad greens (pages 10 and 11)
Horseradish Vinaigrette or Balsamic Vinaigrette (page 81)
About 2 tablespoons finely grated fresh horseradish or prepared horseradish
About 18 Niçoise olives
Freshly shaved Parmesan cheese, preferably parmigiano-reggiano

Apple, Ham, and Cheese Salad

Whether you choose tart or sweet apples, be sure they are crisp and juicy. For a lighter salad, omit the ham.

Make this salad the day before serving to allow flavors to develop.

Prepare the dressing and set aside.

Quarter and core the apples; peel if desired. Using a sharp knife, coarsely chop or cube the apples and place the pieces in a large bowl. Add 2 tablespoons of the lemon juice and toss well to prevent the apples from discoloring. Drain and discard the lemon juice. Add the cheese, chopped fennel or celery, ham, currants or raisins, and dressing to the apples and toss well.

Just before serving, garnish with the mint or fennel sprigs or celery leaves.

Serves 6 as a salad course, or 3 or 4 as a main course.

Nonfat Yogurt Dressing (page 86)
4 large crisp apples
2 tablespoons freshly squeezed lemon juice
8 ounces firm smooth cheese such as Cheddar, Emmenthaler, or Gouda, cut into ¼-inch cubes
1¼ cups chopped fennel or celery
1 pound flavorful baked ham, sliced ½ inch thick and then cut into cubes
¼ cup dried currants or raisins, plumped in hot water for 15 minutes and drained
Fresh mint or fennel sprigs or celery leaves for garnish

Tropical Fruit Salad with Passion Fruit Dressing

Add or substitute other tropical fruits for those suggested here. If you wish, serve the dressing in hollowed-out passion-fruit shells alongside the sliced fruits.

To toast the coconut, place it in a skillet over medium-high heat and stir constantly until lightly golden and fragrant, about 2 minutes. Transfer to a plate to cool; set aside.

Prepare the dressing and set aside. Reserve passion fruit shells to hold dressing, if desired.

In a large bowl, combine all the sliced fruits. Add the dressing and toss well. Sprinkle with the toasted coconut and macadamia nuts. Alternatively, arrange the sliced fruits on individual plates or on a serving platter. Sprinkle with the toasted coconut and macadamia nuts. Drizzle some of the dressing over the top. Pour the remainder of the dressing into hollowed-out passion-fruit shells, if desired, or into an attractive bowl and position alongside the fruit. Garnish rims of the plates or platter with the pineapple leaves and flowers (if used).

Serves 6 to 8 as a salad course, or 3 or 4 as a light main course.

1 cup shredded fresh or dried coconut
Passion Fruit Dressing (page 89)
2 ripe mangoes, peeled, pitted, and sliced
2 medium-sized ripe papayas, peeled, seeded, and sliced
1 small ripe pineapple, peeled, cored, and sliced
3 medium-sized bananas, peeled, sliced, and tossed in about 1 tablespoon freshly squeezed lemon juice to prevent discoloring
2 starfruits, sliced
2 or 3 kiwifruits, peeled and sliced
1 cup (about 4 ounces) unsalted roasted macadamia nuts
Leaves from pineapple top for plate garnish (optional)
Pesticide-free, nontoxic tropical flowers such as plumaria or miniature orchids for plate garnish (optional)

Moroccan Fruit and Nut Salad

1 head romaine lettuce, tough outer
leaves discarded
1 head Belgian endive
½ cup walnuts, oven toasted (page 90)
½ cup slivered almonds, oven toasted
(page 90)
4 large navel and/or blood oranges
½ cup freshly squeezed orange juice
3 tablespoons freshly squeezed
lemon juice
2 tablespoons orange flower water
3 tablespoons sugar
About ⅛ teaspoon salt
½ teaspoon ground cinnamon
3 tablespoons walnut oil
1 cup fresh mint leaves
½ cup chopped dates
Pesticide-free rose petals for garnish
(optional)

An exotic change of pace that goes well with a spicy meal. Or serve in place of a more conventional dessert; a piece of creamy cheese such as a triple crème goes great with the fruit if you wish a richer ending to a meal.

Wash, dry, and chill the lettuce and endive as described on page 10.

Toast the walnuts and almonds and set aside.

Peel the oranges, removing all white pith. Cut between the segments and remove the membranes and seeds. Place the segments in a bowl.

In a small bowl, combine the orange juice, lemon juice, orange flower water, sugar, salt to taste, cinnamon, and walnut oil. Mix well and set aside.

In a large bowl, combine the chilled lettuce, endive, and mint leaves and toss with the dressing to taste. Transfer the greens mixture to a large platter or individual plates. Top the greens with the orange segments and sprinkle with the dates and toasted nuts. Garnish with rose petals (if used).

Serves 6 to 8 as a salad course or light dessert.

DRESSINGS
&TOPPINGS

Basic Vinaigrette

The proportions of vinegar and oil in classic "French dressing" are a matter of personal taste. Most recipes call for one part acid to three parts oil. I prefer one part acid to two parts oil; weight watchers and those who enjoy a tart dressing may choose to use equal parts. Since acidity varies with the vinegar or citrus juice used, adjust the accompanying recipe to suit your taste and the intensity of the ingredients.

Consider the wide range of potential acids, used alone or in combination: freshly squeezed lemon or lime juice, white wine vinegar or red wine vinegar, cider vinegar, balsamic vinegar, champagne vinegar, sherry vinegar, or any of a number of Asian rice vinegars. It is usually best to avoid vinegars that are preflavored with garlic, herbs, or other seasonings; add your own fresh flavorings when you prepare the dressing.

Likewise, there are numerous oils from which to choose. If you like a light-tasting dressing, choose a high-quality vegetable oil such as canola or safflower. For a richer flavor, choose a light to fruity olive oil. This is no time to skimp on quality, since the oil remains uncooked; choose a virgin or cold-pressed oil for optimal flavor. Sometimes it is best to blend oils for a more complex flavor. For example, a little Asian-style sesame oil adds a rich flavor to plain vegetable oil.

Fresh herbs, vegetables, spices, and mustards offer countless possibilities for vinaigrette variations. Members of the onion family—garlic, onions, shallots, green onions, and leeks—enhance almost any dressing. Sweet peppers and fiery chiles add both color and zest. And don't forget the other "zest": Add minced lemon, lime, orange, tangerine, or grapefruit peel; be sure to use only the colored portion, never the bitter white pith.

Here is a basic combination to get you started. A number of variations follow. Should you end up with a dressing that tastes too strong, dilute it with a little water to taste.

For a warm vinaigrette to serve over wilted greens or meat salads, combine the oil and all other ingredients, except the vinegar or citrus juice. Place over medium heat or in a microwave until the mixture is hot, 1 to 2 minutes. Remove from the heat and let cool for about 30 seconds, then slowly whisk in or stir in the vinegar or citrus juice. Serve immediately.

⅓ cup vinegar or freshly squeezed lemon or lime juice, or a combination of vinegar and citrus juice
About 1 teaspoon sugar (optional)
About ½ teaspoon salt
About ½ teaspoon freshly ground black pepper
⅔ cup fruity olive oil, preferably extra-virgin

In a bowl or a jar with a cover, combine the vinegar or juice, sugar (if used), and salt and pepper to taste. Whisk well or cover and shake to blend well. Add the oil and whisk or shake until emulsified. Alternatively, the ingredients may be mixed in a food processor or a blender. Use immediately or let stand at room temperature for as long as overnight.

Makes about 1 cup.

VINAIGRETTE VARIATIONS

Using the preceding recipe for Basic Vinaigrette, make the following substitutions or additions.

Asian-Style Vinaigrette. Use rice wine vinegar. Add ¼ cup soy sauce (preferably tamari), 1 tablespoon minced fresh ginger root, and 1 teaspoon minced or pressed garlic (or 2 whole garlic cloves if using a food processor or a blender). Use equal parts Asian-style sesame oil, high-quality vegetable oil, and hot chile oil.

Balsamic Vinaigrette. Use balsamic vinegar. Add ½ teaspoon minced or pressed garlic (or 1 whole clove if using a food processor or a blender) and 1 tablespoon Dijon-style mustard. Use extra-virgin olive oil.

Berry Vinaigrette. Use blueberry-, raspberry-, or strawberry-flavored vinegar. Add a little ground cinnamon to taste and about ¼ cup crushed fresh or thawed frozen berries (same as the flavor of the vinegar). Use equal parts olive oil and high-quality vegetable oil. Blend in a food processor or a blender.

Cheese Vinaigrette. Stir in about 3 tablespoons crumbled blue cheese or goat's cheese or freshly grated Parmesan cheese, preferably parmigiano-reggiano.

Citrus Vinaigrette. Use freshly squeezed lemon, lime, grapefruit, orange, or tangerine juice. Add about 1 tablespoon freshly grated or minced citrus zest from the same fruit. Use olive oil or high-quality vegetable oil.

Creamy Vinaigrette. Use cider vinegar. Add ½ teaspoon dry mustard and ¼ cup heavy (whipping) cream or canned evaporated milk. Use high-quality vegetable oil.

Curried Vinaigrette. Use freshly squeezed lemon juice. Add 1 teaspoon grated fresh ginger root, 1 teaspoon minced or pressed garlic (or 2 whole garlic cloves if using a food processor or a blender), 1 teaspoon high-quality curry powder, and ½ teaspoon dry mustard. Use high-quality vegetable oil.

Hazelnut Vinaigrette. Use white wine vinegar or sherry vinegar. Add 1 teaspoon Dijon-style mustard. Use equal parts hazelnut oil and light olive oil. Stir in 2 tablespoons finely chopped, oven-toasted hazelnuts if desired.

Herb Vinaigrette. Use balsamic vinegar, wine vinegar, or freshly squeezed lemon juice. Add 1 teaspoon minced or pressed garlic (or 2 whole garlic cloves if using a food processor or a blender) and about ¼ cup minced fresh basil, chives, cilantro (coriander), dill, mint, or tarragon, or use a pleasing combination of herbs. When fresh herbs are unavailable, add 1½ tablespoons crumbled dried herbs, or to taste. Use extra-virgin olive oil.

Horseradish Vinaigrette. Use red or white wine vinegar. Add 1 tablespoon horseradish, preferably freshly grated, or to taste. Use extra-virgin olive oil.

Hot Chile Vinaigrette. Use red wine vinegar or freshly squeezed lime juice. Add 1 tablespoon minced fresh jalapeño or other hot chile pepper, or to taste, and 3 tablespoons minced fresh cilantro (coriander). Use light olive oil or high-quality vegetable oil.

Mustard Vinaigrette. Use balsamic vinegar, wine vinegar, or freshly squeezed lemon juice. Add 1 tablespoon Dijon-style or other favorite mustard and 1 teaspoon minced or pressed garlic (or 2 garlic cloves if using a food processor or a blender). Include the optional sugar. Use extra-virgin olive oil.

Orange Vinaigrette. Use equal parts sherry and balsamic vinegars. Add 1 tablespoon orange-flavored liqueur, 2 tablespoons freshly squeezed orange juice, and 1 tablespoon minced fresh thyme or ½ teaspoon crumbled dried thyme. Use light olive oil or high-quality vegetable oil.

Seed Vinaigrette. Use cider vinegar or freshly squeezed citrus juice. Add 3 tablespoons sesame seeds or poppy seeds, 1½ teaspoons minced yellow onion, ¼ teaspoon Worcestershire sauce, and ¼ teaspoon paprika. Use high-quality vegetable oil. If serving over fruit, increase the sugar to ¼ cup and omit onion and Worcestershire sauce.

Smoked Chile Vinaigrette. Use red wine vinegar, cider vinegar, or freshly squeezed lime juice. Add 2 canned *chiles chipotles* in adobo sauce (from Spanish markets or supermarket ethnic shelves), minced, and about 1 tablespoon of the sauce from the chiles. Use high-quality vegetable oil.

Sun-Dried Tomato Vinaigrette. Use balsamic vinegar. Add 1 tablespoon minced shallot, 1 teaspoon minced or pressed garlic (or 2 garlic cloves if using a food processor or a blender), 8 sun-dried tomatoes (preferably packed in olive oil and drained), and 8 to 10 fresh basil leaves. Use extra-virgin olive oil and a little oil from the tomatoes (if oil-packed tomatoes are used). Blend in a food processor or a blender.

Walnut Vinaigrette. Use sherry vinegar or red wine vinegar. Add about 2 tablespoons finely chopped oven-toasted walnuts (page 90) and 2 tablespoons minced shallot or fresh chives. Use 2 parts walnut oil to 1 part high-quality vegetable oil.

American Mustard Dressing

The idea for this light-tasting variation vinaigrette came from San Francisco cook Elena Solares, who makes it in quantity and keeps it handy in the refrigerator for up to several weeks. I especially enjoy it over cooked beets, broccoli, or other vegetables.

A lemon reamer makes extracting juice from onions easy.

1 cup distilled white vinegar
1 tablespoon dry mustard
2 teaspoons prepared spicy brown mustard
¼ cup fresh white or yellow onion juice
1 teaspoon minced or pressed garlic, or 2 whole garlic cloves if using a food processor or a blender
1 cup olive oil or corn oil
About 1 tablespoon sugar
About ⅛ teaspoon salt
About 1 teaspoon freshly ground black pepper

In a small bowl or a jar with a cover, combine about 2 tablespoons of the vinegar with the dry mustard and whisk well, or cover and shake to liquefy the mustard. Add the remaining vinegar, the brown mustard, onion juice, garlic, and oil and whisk or shake to mix well. Season to taste with sugar, salt, and pepper. Alternatively, combine all the ingredients in a food processor or a blender and blend well. Use immediately, or cover and refrigerate for up to 2 weeks; return to room temperature before using.

Makes about 2 cups.

Moroccan-Style Dressing

Equally good over a single lightly cooked vegetable, a combination of vegetables, or mixed greens.

2 teaspoons minced or pressed garlic, or 2 whole garlic cloves if using a food processor or a blender
¼ cup freshly squeezed lemon juice
1½ teaspoons ground cumin
½ cup minced fresh cilantro (coriander)
⅔ cup fruity olive oil, preferably extra-virgin
About 1 teaspoon salt
About ½ teaspoon freshly ground black pepper

In a small bowl or a jar with a cover, combine all the ingredients, including the salt and pepper to taste, and whisk or shake to blend well. Alternatively, combine all the ingredients in a food processor or a blender, and blend well. Use immediately, or cover and refrigerate for up to 5 days; return to room temperature before using.

Makes about 1 cup.

Warm Onion Dressing

While still warm, pour the dressing over greens, toss to wilt, and sprinkle with crisp bacon.

⅔ cup fruity olive oil, preferably extra-virgin
2 cups thinly sliced yellow onion
2 teaspoons minced or pressed garlic
3 tablespoons cider vinegar
About ½ teaspoon salt
About 1 teaspoon freshly ground black pepper

In a sauté pan, heat 2 tablespoons of the oil over medium-low heat. Add the onion and cook, stirring frequently, until golden brown, 15 to 20 minutes. Add the garlic and cook about 2 minutes longer.

Transfer the onion mixture to a food processor or a blender. Add the remaining oil, the vinegar, and salt and pepper to taste. Blend well. Use immediately, or cool to room temperature, cover, and refrigerate for up to 1 week; reheat before using.

Makes about 1 cup.

Warm Pancetta Dressing

I enjoy this scrumptious combination over mixed greens, including some bitter ones, and fresh figs, strawberries, or sliced pears.

¼ cup fruity olive oil, preferably extra-virgin
5 ounces pancetta (Italian unsmoked bacon) or smoked bacon, coarsely chopped
2 tablespoons pine nuts
3 tablespoons minced fresh basil
1 tablespoon minced fresh lavender flowers, or 1 teaspoon crumbled dried lavender flowers
¼ cup balsamic vinegar or red wine vinegar
About ¼ teaspoon salt
About ½ teaspoon freshly ground black pepper

In a sauté pan or a skillet, heat the oil over medium-high heat. Add the pancetta or bacon and cook, stirring frequently, until browned and crisp, 6 to 7 minutes. Stir in the pine nuts, basil, and lavender and heat through.

Remove from the heat and stir in the vinegar. Season to taste with salt and a generous amount of pepper. Use immediately, or cool to room temperature, cover and refrigerate for up to 1 day; reheat before using.

Makes about ¾ cup.

Spicy Sausage Dressing

Delicious over sliced tomatoes or mixed greens. To serve as a warm dressing, heat the mixture just before using.

3 ounces highly seasoned smoked sausage such as andouille or kielbasa, finely diced
2 tablespoons minced shallot or red onion
½ teaspoon minced or pressed garlic
¾ cup high-quality vegetable oil
1 teaspoon Creole or Dijon-style mustard
½ teaspoon sugar
3 tablespoons red wine vinegar
About 1 teaspoon Tabasco sauce or other hot-pepper sauce
About ¼ teaspoon salt
About ¼ teaspoon freshly ground black pepper

Heat a sauté pan or a skillet over medium heat. Add the sausage and sauté until the fat is rendered. Add the shallot or onion and sauté until the onion is soft, about 4 minutes. Stir in the garlic and sauté about 1 minute longer. Strain and discard the fat. Transfer the sausage mixture to a bowl and cool for about 1 minute.

Whisk or stir the oil, mustard, sugar, vinegar, and pepper sauce, salt, and pepper to taste into the sausage mixture. Serve immediately, or cover and refrigerate for up to 4 days; return to room temperature before using.

Makes about 1 cup.

Creamy Fresh Herb Dressing

In addition to complementing seafood salads, this simple combination enhances potato salad.

1 cup crème fraîche, sour cream, or plain yogurt
1 cup minced mixed fresh herbs such as chervil, chives, dill, and parsley
2 teaspoons freshly squeezed lemon juice, or to taste
About ½ teaspoon salt
About ⅛ teaspoon freshly ground black pepper

In a small bowl, combine all the ingredients, including the salt and pepper to taste and blend well. Let stand at room temperature for about 15 minutes, or cover and refrigerate for up to 4 days; return to room temperature before using.

Makes about 1 cup.

Creamy Cheese Dressing

I prefer to crumble cheese over the top of a salad and then toss the whole salad in vinaigrette. But if you enjoy rich, creamy cheese dressings, be sure to try this one. It uses either goat's milk cheese or the more traditional blue-veined cheese.

3 ounces creamy goat's milk cheese, or 4 ounces creamy blue cheese
1 cup heavy (whipping) cream
3 tablespoons minced fresh chives
1½ teaspoons Dijon-style mustard
About ½ teaspoon salt
About ¼ teaspoon freshly ground white pepper

In a small bowl, food processor, or blender, combine the cheese, cream, chives, and mustard. Whisk or blend until smooth. Season to taste with salt and pepper.

Cover and refrigerate at least 6 hours or for up to 1 week to develop the flavors. Return to room temperature and whisk to smooth just before serving.

Makes about 1¼ cups.

Creamy Onion Dressing

Babs Retzer, one of the best cooks in Marysville, California, serves this over a combination of spinach and lettuce leaves tossed with slivers of sweet red pepper and showers the top with Sesame Cheese Sprinkles (page 91).

½ cup Mayonnaise (page 85) or high-quality commercial mayonnaise
1 cup sour cream
1 tablespoon red or white wine vinegar
1 tablespoon sugar
1 tablespoon minced yellow onion, or 2 tablespoons coarsely chopped yellow onion if using a food processor or a blender
1 teaspoon minced or pressed garlic, or 2 garlic cloves if using a food processor or a blender
About ¾ teaspoon salt

In a small bowl, combine all the ingredients, including the salt to taste, and whisk to blend well. Alternatively, combine all the ingredients in a food processor or a blender and blend well. Let stand about 15 minutes, or cover and refrigerate for up to 1 week; return almost to room temperature before using.

Makes about 1½ cups.

Mayonnaise

I tend to agree with whoever described mayonnaise as "fat at its finest." Use alone to dress a salad or as the base for a creamy dressing. Garlic or fresh herbs may be added to taste. For Italian *maionese,* use all olive oil.

1 whole egg, at room temperature
1 egg yolk, at room temperature
1½ teaspoons Dijon-style mustard
1½ tablespoons freshly squeezed lemon juice or white wine vinegar
1 cup safflower oil or other high-quality vegetable oil, or part olive oil, preferably extra-virgin
About ½ teaspoon salt

In a food processor or a blender, combine the egg, egg yolk, mustard, and lemon juice or vinegar. Blend at high speed for about 30 seconds. With the motor running, add the oil in a slow, steady stream. When the mayonnaise thickens to proper consistency, turn the motor off. With a rubber or plastic spatula, scrape down any oil clinging to the sides of the container and mix gently into the mayonnaise. Add the salt to taste. Use immediately, or cover and refrigerate for up to 1 week; return almost to room temperature before using.

Makes about 1¼ cups.

Buttermilk Dressing

In the last few years, many Americans have become enamored with the tangy flavor of old-fashioned "ranch" dressing. Use with mixed vegetables or potato salad.

½ cup Mayonnaise (adjacent recipe) or high-quality commercial mayonnaise
½ cup buttermilk
1 tablespoon minced fresh chives or green onion, including some green tops
½ teaspoon minced or pressed garlic, or 1 whole garlic clove if using a food processor or a blender
2 teaspoons minced fresh parsley
About ¼ teaspoon salt
About ¼ teaspoon freshly ground black pepper
About ⅛ teaspoon ground dried red chile or hot-pepper sauce

In a small bowl, a jar with a cover, a food processor, or a blender, combine all the ingredients, including the salt, pepper, and ground chile or hot-pepper sauce to taste. Whisk, shake, or blend until smooth. Transfer the mixture to a bowl, cover, and refrigerate for at least 1 hour or for up to 4 days. Return almost to room temperature before using.

Makes about 1 cup.

BACON VARIATION: Cut 3 or 4 bacon slices into ½-inch lengths and cook until crisp. Using a slotted utensil, transfer the bacon to paper toweling to drain and cool. Stir the bacon into the finished dressing.

Avocado Dressing

Serve this smooth dressing with crisp head lettuce, mixed vegetables, seafood, or meat salads. For a spicier dressing, add chili powder and Tabasco sauce or other hot-pepper sauce to taste.

1 large ripe avocado, halved and pitted
3 tablespoons grated yellow or red onion
2 tablespoons freshly squeezed lime or lemon juice
1 tablespoon Worcestershire sauce
1 cup crème fraîche, sour cream, plain yogurt, or mayonnaise
About ½ teaspoon salt
About ¼ teaspoon freshly ground black pepper

Scrape the avocado pulp into a food processor or a blender and discard the skin. Add the onion, lime or lemon juice, Worcestershire sauce, and crème fraîche, sour cream, yogurt, or mayonnaise and blend until smooth. Season to taste with salt and pepper. Use immediately, or cover and refrigerate for up to 1 day; return almost to room temperature before using.

Makes about 1½ cups.

Low-Fat Dressing

When you're reducing fat intake, try this flavorful alternative to high-calorie combinations on your favorite leafy salads.

¼ cup red wine vinegar
2 teaspoons freshly squeezed lemon juice
1½ teaspoons Dijon-style mustard
1 teaspoon sugar
½ teaspoon minced or pressed garlic, or 1 whole garlic clove if using a food processor or a blender
1½ tablespoons chopped fresh basil, oregano, tarragon, or other herb of choice, or a pleasing combination, or 2 teaspoons crumbled dried herbs
1 teaspoon Worcestershire sauce
2 tablespoons canola oil or other high-quality vegetable oil
½ cup water
About ¼ teaspoon salt
About ⅛ teaspoon freshly ground black pepper

In a small bowl, a jar with a cover, a food processor, or a blender, combine the vinegar, lemon juice, mustard, sugar, garlic, herbs, and Worcestershire sauce. Whisk, shake, or blend well. Mix in the oil and water and season to taste with salt and pepper. Cover and refrigerate at least overnight, or for up to 1 week; return to room temperature before serving.

Makes about 1 cup.

Nonfat Yogurt Dressing

Good with almost any salad that calls for a light touch. If calories aren't a problem, substitute mayonnaise for part of the yogurt. For a more flavorful dressing, add minced or pressed garlic and/or ground dried red chile to taste.

1 cup plain nonfat yogurt
2 tablespoons freshly squeezed lemon or lime juice
1 tablespoon minced fresh chervil, dill, parsley, mint, or other herb of choice, or a pleasing combination
About ½ teaspoon salt
About ¼ teaspoon freshly ground black pepper

In a small bowl, a food processor, or a blender, whisk or blend the yogurt until smooth. Add the remaining ingredients, including the salt and pepper to taste, and mix well. Let stand for 15 minutes, or cover and refrigerate for up to 1 week; return to room temperature before serving.

Makes 1 cup.

MIDDLE EASTERN VARIATION:
Add ½ teaspoon minced or pressed garlic, ¼ teaspoon ground cumin, and ground cayenne pepper to taste. Use fresh mint for the herb.

Tahini Dressing

½ teaspoon minced or pressed garlic, or 1 whole garlic clove if using a food processor or a blender
½ cup sesame paste *(tahini)*
¼ cup olive oil
½ cup freshly squeezed lemon juice
3 tablespoons coarsely chopped fresh mint or parsley, preferably flat-leaf type
About 1 teaspoon salt
About ½ teaspoon freshly ground black pepper
About ¼ cup water

In a small bowl, a food processor, or a blender, combine the garlic, sesame paste, oil, lemon juice, mint or parsley, and salt and pepper to taste. Whisk, shake, or blend well. Mix in just enough water until the dressing is the consistency of heavy cream. Use immediately, or cover and refrigerate for up to 4 days; return to room temperature before using.

Makes about 1 cup.

Japanese Sesame Dressing

Use over lightly steamed spinach, green beans, or other barely cooked vegetables. Sprinkle the salad with toasted sesame seeds (page 91). Japanese fish stock base can be purchased at Asian groceries and well-stocked supermarkets.

⅓ cup soy sauce, preferably tamari
⅓ cup Asian-style sesame oil
¼ cup sugar
¼ cup Japanese fish stock *(dashi)*, homemade chicken stock, or canned chicken broth
Hot chile oil

In a small saucepan, combine all the ingredients, including the chile oil to taste. Place over low heat and stir until the sugar is dissolved. Alternatively, combine the ingredients in a small bowl and heat in a microwave oven until the sugar is dissolved. Cool to room temperature and use immediately, or cover and refrigerate for up to 1 week; return to room temperature before using.

Makes about 1 cup.

Creamy Japanese Dressing

Although not authentically Japanese, this dressing is similar to a sauce that was served with *mizutaki* in a favorite San Francisco Japanese restaurant. It makes an interesting dressing for crisp greens, cold noodles or rice, lightly cooked vegetables, or poached chicken.

1¼ cups Mayonnaise (page 85) or high-quality commercial mayonnaise
¾ cup sour cream
⅓ cup homemade beef stock or canned beef broth
2 tablespoons soy sauce, preferably tamari
2 tablespoons sake
1 teaspoon minced or pressed garlic, or 2 whole garlic cloves if using a food processor or blender
About 1¾ teaspoons sugar
About 1 tablespoon freshly ground black pepper

In a bowl, a food processor, or a blender, whisk or blend all the ingredients, including sugar and pepper to taste; be generous with the pepper. Cover and refrigerate for at least 1 hour or for up to 1 week; return almost to room temperature before using.

Makes about 2½ cups.

Thai-Style Dressing

Fiery chile paste or oil can be found in Asian markets or the ethnic sections of some supermarkets. Spoon this tangy dressing over a simple mixture of cucumber and red onion and top with chopped fresh cilantro (coriander).

⅓ cup sugar
⅓ cup boiling water
⅓ cup rice vinegar
1 teaspoon minced or pressed garlic
About ½ teaspoon Thai chile paste or Asian hot chile oil
About ½ teaspoon salt

In a small bowl or jar with a cover, combine the sugar and water and stir or shake until the sugar is dissolved. Add all the remaining ingredients, including the chile paste or oil and salt to taste.

Cool the dressing to room temperature before using, or cover and refrigerate for up to 1 week; return to room temperature before using.

Makes about 1 cup.

Southeast Asian Lime Dressing

Try this chile-laced dressing with mixed greens and cooked meat or seafood.

2 tablespoons safflower oil or other high-quality vegetable oil
1 tablespoon minced or pressed garlic
3 tablespoons coarsely chopped fresh red or green hot chiles such as Serrano, or 1 tablespoon crushed dried red hot chile
½ cup freshly squeezed lime juice
¼ cup fish sauce, preferably Thai (nam pla), or 2 tablespoons soy sauce
2 tablespoons sugar

In a small saucepan, heat the oil over medium heat. Add the garlic and cook until soft but not browned, about 1 minute. Transfer the garlic and oil to a food processor or a blender. Add all the remaining ingredients and blend until smooth. Use immediately, or cover and refrigerate for up to 2 weeks; return to room temperature before using.

Makes about 1 cup.

Indonesian Peanut Dressing

Traditionally served with mixed raw or cooked vegetables, this complex salad topping is also good with cooled pasta and chicken, meat, or shellfish.

Look for the exotic ingredients in markets that sell foods from Southeast Asia.

½ cup preserved tamarind pulp, or 3 tablespoons tamarind concentrate or freshly squeezed lemon juice
½ cup warm water, if using tamarind pulp
2 tablespoons coarsely chopped fresh green hot chiles
½ stalk lemon grass, bottom portion only, coarsely chopped, or 1 teaspoon minced lemon zest
3 thin slices fresh galangal root or ginger root
2 tablespoons coarsely chopped yellow onion
6 whole garlic cloves
½ teaspoon shrimp paste (optional)
1½ cups roasted peanuts, ground
1 teaspoon cumin seed
1½ teaspoons coriander seed
¼ cup cold water
2 tablespoons peanut oil or other high-quality vegetable oil
3 cups fresh or canned coconut milk
3 tablespoons fish sauce, preferably Indonesian (petis), or 1½ tablespoons soy sauce
¼ cup sugar

If using the tamarind pulp, place it in a small bowl and add the warm water; let stand until soft, about 15 minutes. With the back of a spoon, press the pulp through a fine-mesh sieve, being sure to press through as much pulp as possible. Scrape the outside of the sieve to retrieve all the pulp and set aside; discard the residue. If using the tamarind concentrate or lemon juice, reserve.

In a food processor or a blender, combine the chiles, lemon grass, galangal or ginger, onion, garlic, shrimp paste (if used), peanuts, cumin and coriander seed, and cold water. Blend to a smooth paste.

In a skillet or a saucepan, heat the oil over medium heat. Add the chile paste and cook, stirring constantly, until fragrant and deep in color, 2 to 3 minutes. Stir in the coconut milk, a little at a time, until the mixture is smooth and slightly thickened. Add the reserved tamarind liquid or lemon juice, fish sauce or soy sauce, and sugar and bring to a boil, stirring to dissolve sugar. Remove from the heat and let stand to cool to room temperature.

Use the dressing immediately, or cover and store for up to several weeks; return it to room temperature before using. If the dressing becomes too thick, stir in a little warm water to return it to a pourable consistency.

Makes about 3½ cups.

Papaya-Seed Dressing

Papaya seeds add a peppery crunch to this dressing, which is not only good over fruit, but also with cold chicken or other meats.

⅓ cup white wine vinegar
1 tablespoon grated yellow onion
2 teaspoons Dijon-style mustard
2 tablespoons sugar, or to taste
About ½ teaspoon salt
About 2 teaspoons Tabasco sauce
    or other hot-pepper sauce
⅔ cup canola oil or other high-
    quality vegetable oil
2 tablespoons papaya seeds

In a food processor or a blender, combine the vinegar, onion, mustard, sugar, and salt and pepper sauce to taste. Mix well. With the motor running, slowly drizzle in the oil until the mixture emulsifies. Add the papaya seeds and blend just until the seeds are coarsely chopped. Use immediately, or cover and refrigerate for up to 1 week; bring to room temperature before using.

Makes about 1 cup.

Honey Dressing

Excellent over fresh fruit or a mixture of fruit and greens.

⅔ cup sugar
1 teaspoon dry mustard
1 teaspoon paprika
1 teaspoon celery seed
About ¼ teaspoon salt
1 teaspoon grated white or yellow
    onion
⅓ cup cider vinegar
⅓ cup honey
1 cup canola oil or other high-
    quality vegetable oil

In a small bowl, a food processor, or a blender, combine the sugar, mustard, paprika, celery seed, salt, onion, vinegar, and honey. Whisk or blend well. If using a bowl, slowly beat in the oil until the mixture emulsifies. If using a blender or a food processor, engage the motor and slowly drizzle in the oil, blending until the mixture emulsifies. Use immediately, or cover and refrigerate for up to 1 week; return to room temperature and stir to blend before using.

Makes about 2 cups.

Passion Fruit Dressing

Delicious over tropical fruits. The passion fruits should be soft and shriveled before using.

8 medium-sized passion fruits
3 tablespoons freshly squeezed
    orange juice
1 tablespoon freshly squeezed
    lemon or lime juice
1½ tablespoons sugar
5 tablespoons canola oil or other
    high-quality vegetable oil

Cut off the stem end of each passion fruit and scoop the pulp into a fine-mesh sieve set over a nonreactive bowl. With the back of a spoon, press against the pulp to extract the juice; discard the pulp and seeds. Transfer the juice to a small bowl, a jar with a cover, a food processor, or a blender.

Add the orange and lemon or lime juices, sugar, and oil to the passion fruit juice. Mix well. Use immediately, or cover and refrigerate for up to 1 day; return to room temperature before using.

Makes about 1 cup.

Sweet Crunchy Nuts

Whether left as halves or chopped, these sweet, crisp nuts are delicious sprinkled over a green salad.

3 cups water
1 cup walnut or pecan halves, or
coarsely chopped
2 tablespoons sugar
Peanut oil or other high-quality
vegetable oil for deep-frying
Salt

Place the water in a saucepan over high heat and bring to a boil. Add the nuts, return to a boil, and cook for 1 minute. Drain the nuts, rinse under running warm water, and drain again. Transfer the warm nuts to a bowl, pour the sugar over the nuts, and stir until the sugar is dissolved.

In a saucepan, pour the oil to a depth of 1 inch. Heat to 360° F, or until a small cube of bread turns lightly golden within seconds of being dropped into the oil. Using a slotted utensil, transfer the nuts to the oil and cook, stirring frequently, until golden, about 3 minutes; watch carefully to prevent burning. Again using a slotted utensil, transfer the nuts to a colander set over a bowl or in the sink and season to taste with salt. Lightly stir for about 5 minutes to keep the nuts from sticking together. Pour the nuts onto a plate to cool completely. The fried nuts may be stored in a tightly covered container for up to 2 weeks.

Makes 1 cup.

Oven-Toasted Nuts

Be sure that the nuts you use are fresh. Toast only as many as you need, as they will turn rancid quickly.

Shelled cashews, hazelnuts
(filberts), macadamia, pecans,
walnuts, or other nuts

Preheat an oven to 350° F.

Spread the nuts in a single layer in an ovenproof skillet or on a baking sheet. Toast in the preheated oven, stirring occasionally, until lightly browned and fragrant, 10 to 15 minutes. Transfer to a plate to cool.

To remove the skins from hazelnuts, place the warm nuts in a coarse cloth towel and rub to remove the loose skins; don't worry about bits of skin that stick to the nuts.

Pan-Toasted Seeds or Nuts

Toasted nuts add nutritious crunch and flavor when sprinkled over or tossed into salads.

Pumpkin seeds, sesame seeds, sunflower seeds, almonds, cashews, pine nuts, or peanuts

Place the seeds or nuts in a small, heavy skillet over medium heat. Toast, shaking the pan or stirring frequently, until the seeds or nuts are lightly golden and fragrant, about 5 minutes. Pour onto a plate to cool.

Makes 1 cup.

Crispy Bacon Bits

Freshly made bits of crisp bacon are much more flavorful than their commercial counterparts. Prepare only as much as you need for serving, as bacon loses its crispness quickly.

½ pound sliced or slab smoked bacon or pancetta (Italian unsmoked bacon)

Cut sliced bacon crosswise into pieces about ½ inch wide. If using slab bacon, cut into ¼-inch dice.

Heat a heavy skillet over medium heat. Add the bacon, and cook, stirring frequently, until browned and crisp, 6 to 7 minutes. Using a slotted utensil, transfer the bacon to paper toweling to drain.

Makes about 1 cup.

Sesame Cheese Sprinkles

Cooking teacher Babs Retzer introduced me to this topping, which she strews over spinach and crisp lettuce tossed in Creamy Onion Dressing (page 84).

2 tablespoons unsalted butter or olive oil
1 cup sesame seeds
½ cup freshly grated Parmesan cheese, preferably parmigiano-reggiano

In a skillet or a saucepan, melt the butter or heat the oil over medium-low heat. Add the sesame seeds and cook until golden, about 3 minutes. Transfer to a bowl to cool, then stir in the cheese. Use immediately, or cover tightly for up to 2 days.

Makes about 1½ cups.

Croutons

For a change from the ubiquitous cube-shaped crouton, cut skinny baguettes into thin slices.

½ cup (1 stick) unsalted butter
About ½ cup fruity olive oil, preferably extra-virgin
2 tablespoons minced or pressed garlic, or to taste (optional)
4 cups day-old bread, preferably French style, cut into ¾-inch cubes

In a large sauté pan or skillet, melt the butter with the oil over medium-low heat. Add the garlic (if used) and bread and toss until the bread pieces are well coated. Reduce the heat to low (or transfer to a preheated 350° F oven) and cook, stirring or turning frequently, until the bread is golden on all sides, about 20 minutes. Transfer the bread to paper toweling to drain and cool slightly. Use immediately, or cool completely, then store in an airtight container for up to 1 day.

Makes 4 cups.

HERB VARIATION: Add 3 tablespoons minced fresh herbs of choice, or more to taste, or 1 tablespoon crumbled dried herbs of choice along with the bread.

Polenta Croutons

Use as you would croutons.

½ cup coarse yellow cornmeal
½ teaspoon salt, or to taste
2½ cups water
2 tablespoons unsalted butter, at room temperature
About ½ cup fine yellow cornmeal for dusting
About ½ cup corn oil

In a heavy saucepan, combine the coarse cornmeal, salt, and water and stir well. Place over medium-high heat and bring to a simmer, stirring occasionally with a wooden spoon. Reduce the heat to low and simmer, stirring frequently and scraping the bottom of the pot with the spoon, until the mixture comes away from the sides of the pan and is quite thick, about 30 minutes. Stir in the butter and pour the mixture into a 12- by 8-inch baking pan. Let stand until cold and firm.

Slice the polenta into 2-inch squares. Toss pieces in the fine cornmeal until lightly coated.

Heat the oil in a sauté pan or a skillet over medium-high heat. Add the polenta pieces, a few at a time, and cook, turning, until lightly browned and crisp all over, about 5 minutes. Using a slotted utensil, transfer the polenta pieces to paper toweling to drain. Use warm or let stand at room temperature for up to 4 hours.

Makes 24 squares.

Crunchy Tortilla Strips

These crisp strips are another excellent stand-in for croutons.

High-quality vegetable oil for deep-frying
3 or 4 corn tortillas or flour tortillas, cut into strips about ⅜ inch wide and 2 or 3 inches long
Salt

In a deep-fat fryer or a deep saucepan, pour in the oil to a depth of about 2 inches. Heat to 365° F, or until a bit of tortilla turns lightly golden within seconds of being dropped in the oil. Drop in the tortilla strips, a few at a time, and fry, stirring frequently, until golden. Using a slotted utensil, transfer the strips to paper toweling to drain. While still hot, sprinkle with salt to taste. Use warm or let cool completely, then store in an airtight container for up to 1 day.

Makes about 3 cups.

Crunchy Pasta

If you don't have fresh pasta, cook dried pasta briefly to soften and drain well, then fry as directed. Scatter the crisp noodles over green salads.

In lieu of frying, the pasta may be tossed with the herbs and cheese, spread on a baking sheet, and baked in a preheated 250° F oven until crisp and golden; stir occasionally.

½ cup minced mixed fresh herbs
    such as oregano, rosemary,
    and sage, or 3 tablespoons
    crumbled mixed dried herbs
½ cup freshly grated Parmesan
    cheese, preferably
    parmigiano-reggiano
Olive oil for deep-frying
8 ounces fresh pasta, cut into
    noodles about 2 inches long
    or into small fanciful shapes
Salt
Freshly ground black pepper or
    ground cayenne pepper

In a small bowl, combine the herbs and cheese, mix well, and set aside.

In a deep-fat fryer or a deep saucepan, pour in the oil to a depth of 2 inches. Heat to 365° F, or until a bit of pasta turns lightly golden within seconds of being dropped in the oil. Drop in the pasta by small handfuls and cook, stirring frequently, until golden brown. Using a slotted utensil, transfer the pasta to paper toweling to drain briefly. While still hot, sprinkle the pasta with the herb-cheese mixture and salt and pepper to taste. Use warm, or cool completely, then store in an airtight container for up to 1 day.

Makes about 3 cups.

Mimosa Topping

Sprinkle this simple combination over green salads to add a festive touch.

2 hard-cooked eggs
3 tablespoons minced fresh herbs
    of choice

Finely chop or grate the egg whites and yolks. In a bowl, combine the eggs and the herbs and mix well. Use immediately, or cover and refrigerate for up to several hours; return to room temperature before using.

Makes about ½ cup.

Tomato Chutney

Serve chilled as an accompaniment to meat salads or add a little to a vinaigrette for tossed greens. To make the chutney in quantity, multiply the recipe, then pack into sterilized jars, seal, and process in a boiling water bath according to canning jar manufacturer's directions.

1½ cups chopped onion
¾ cup cider vinegar
½ cup packed light brown sugar
½ teaspoon ground allspice
¼ teaspoon ground cinnamon
About ½ teaspoon salt
4 whole cloves
4 black peppercorns
2 pounds ripe tomatoes, peeled,
    seeded, if desired, and
    coarsely chopped

In a saucepan, combine the onion, vinegar, sugar, allspice, cinnamon, and salt to taste. Tie the cloves and peppercorns in a cheesecloth bag and add to the mixture. Bring the mixture to a boil over medium-high heat. Cover, reduce the heat to low, and simmer until the onion is tender, about 20 minutes.

Stir in the tomatoes and continue to simmer, uncovered, until most of the liquid evaporates, about 20 minutes. Remove and discard the cheesecloth bag and season to taste with salt. Cool the chutney to room temperature, cover, and refrigerate.

Makes about 1 pint.

RECIPE INDEX

Apple, Ham, and Cheese Salad 73
American Mustard Dressing 82
Asian Noodle Salad 36
Asian-Style Vinaigrette 81
Autumn Roots Salad 24
Avocado Dressing 85

Bacon Bits, Crispy 91
Balsamic Vinaigrette 81
Basic Green Salad 9
Basic Vinaigrette 80
Bean and Corn Salad, Spicy Black 27
Bean Salad with Bresaola,
    Warm White 69
Berry Vinaigrette 81
Bread Salad, Toasted 34
Buttermilk Dressing 85

Cabbage Salad, Lobster and Spicy 43
Caesar Salad with Garlic Croutons 13
California Chinese Duck Salad 61
Cheese Dressing, Creamy 84
Cheese Sprinkles, Sesame 91
Cheese Vinaigrette 81
Chicken and Vegetable Salad,
    Mediterranean Roast 50
Chicken Salad, Green Papaya 56
Chinese Duck Salad, California 61
Chutney, Tomato 93
Citrus Vinaigrette 81
Cobb Salad, Southwestern Style 62
Coleslaw, Peanutty 17
Crab and Melon with Mint Vinaigrette 46
Creamy Cheese Dressing 84
Creamy Fresh Herb Dressing 84
Creamy Japanese Dressing 87
Creamy Onion Dressing 84
Creamy Vinaigrette 81
Crispy Bacon Bits 91
Croutons 92
Crunchy Pasta 93
Crunchy Tortilla Strips 92
Curried Tuna Salad 48
Curried Vinaigrette 81

Duck Salad, California Chinese 61

Eggplant Salad 19

Figs and Arugula with Lavender Dressing,
    Grilled Pancetta-Wrapped 64
Fruit and Nut Salad, Moroccan 76
Fruit, Nuts, and Greens Salad 15
Fruit Salad with Passion Fruit Dressing,
    Tropical 75

Gado-Gado 29
Goat Cheese Salad, Grilled Vegetables
    and 22
Green Papaya Chicken Salad 56
Grilled Pancetta-Wrapped Figs and
    Arugula with Lavender Dressing 64
Grilled Vegetables and Goat Cheese
    Salad 22

Ham, and Cheese Salad, Apple 73
Hazelnut Vinaigrette 81
Herb Dressing, Creamy Fresh 84
Herb Vinaigrette 81
Honey Dressing 89
Horseradish Vinaigrette 81
Hot Chile Vinaigrette 81

Indonesian Peanut Dressing 88
Indonesian Vegetable Salad with Peanut
    Dressing (Gado-Gado) 29

Japanese Dressing, Creamy 87
Japanese Rice and Chicken Salad 53
Japanese Sesame Dressing 87

Lime Dressing, Southeast Asian 88
Lobster and Spicy Cabbage Salad 43
Low-Fat Dressing 86

Mayonnaise 85
Mediterranean Roast Chicken and
    Vegetable Salad 50
Mimosa Topping 93
Mixed Grain and Herb Tabbouleh 38
Moroccan Fruit and Nut Salad 76

Moroccan-Style Dressing 82
Mushroom Salad, Warm Wild 21
Mustard Vinaigrette 81

Nonfat Yogurt Dressing 86
Noodle Salad, Asian 36
Nut-Ball Salad 30
Nuts, Oven-Toasted 90
Nuts, Pan-Toasted Seeds or 91
Nuts, Sweet Crunchy 90

Onion Dressing, Creamy 84
Onion Dressing, Warm 83
Orange Vinaigrette 81
Oven-Toasted Nuts 90

Pancetta Dressing, Warm 83
Pan-Toasted Seeds or Nuts 91
Papaya Chicken Salad, Green 56
Papaya-Seed Dressing 89
Passion Fruit Dressing 89
Pasta, Crunchy 93
Peanut Dressing, Indonesian 88
Peanutty Coleslaw 17
Polenta Croutons 92
Potato Leek Salad with Spicy Sausage
    Dressing 67

Rice and Chicken Salad, Japanese 53

Seafood Salad 40
Seed Vinaigrette 81
Seeds or Nuts, Pan-Toasted 91
Sesame Cheese Sprinkles 91
Sesame Dressing, Japanese 87
Shrimp Salad, Southeast Asian Warm
    Spicy 45
Smoked Chile Vinaigrette 82
Smoked Turkey and Wild Rice Salad 59
Smoked Veal Loin with Tomato Chutney
    and Horseradish 71
Southeast Asian Lime Dressing 88
Southeast Asian Warm Spicy Shrimp
    Salad 45
Southern Fried Salad 55
Spaghetti Squash and Nut Salad 32
Spicy Black Bean and Corn Salad 27

Spicy Sausage Dressing 83
Sun-Dried Tomato Vinaigrette 82
Sweet Crunchy Nuts 90

Tabbouleh, Mixed Grain and Herb 38
Tahini Dressing 86
Thai-Style Dressing 87
Toasted Bread Salad 34
Tomato Chutney 93
Tortilla Strips, Crunchy 92
Tropical Fruit Salad with Passion Fruit
    Dressing 75
Tuna Salad, Curried 48
Turkey and Wild Rice Salad, Smoked 59

Veal Loin with Tomato Chutney and
    Horseradish, Smoked 71
Vinaigrette, Basic 80
Vinaigrette Variations 81–82

Walnut Vinaigrette 82
Warm Onion Dressing 83
Warm Pancetta Dressing 83
Warm White Bean Salad with Bresaola 69
Warm Wild Mushroom Salad 21
Wild Rice Salad, Smoked Turkey and 59

INDEX TO SALAD RECIPES IN OTHER JAMES McNAIR BOOKS

BEEF COOKBOOK:
Sweet and Tangy Beef Salad 23

CHEESE COOKBOOK:
Fontina and Roasted Peppers 44
Potato and Cheese Salad with Chive
    Dressing 42
Tomato and Mozzarella with Basil
    Vinaigrette 42

CHICKEN:
Chicken Salad with Hearts of Artichoke
    and Palm in Garlic Mayonnaise 32
Smoked Chicken Salad with Blueberry
    Dressing 86
Tropical Chicken Salad with Lime
    Dressing 32

COLD CUISINE:
Beef Salad, Thai Style 55
Chicken in Mango Mayonnaise 40
Marinated Squid 28
Mixed Seafood Salad (Fruits de Mer) 25
Spicy Shrimp with Oranges and Mint 27
Wild Rice and Beef in Red Pepper
    Dressing 56

COLD PASTA:
Angel's Hair with Three Caviars 31
Beef Fillet with Macaroni in Shallot-
    Mustard Dressing 74
Bow Ties with Chicken and White
    Vegetables in Garlic Mayonnaise 85
Buckwheat Noodles with Asparagus in
    Sesame Dressing 55
Chicken, Mein, and Vegetables in Creamy
    Szechuan Dressing 67
Corkscrew Pasta with Vegetables in
    Italian Vinaigrette 60
Curly Pasta with Vegetables in Green
    Mexican Salsa 57
Duck Breast and Pasta in Hazelnut-
    Raspberry Dressing 80
Freshly Poached Tuna with Vegetables
    and Pasta Niçoise 69
Macaroni with Tomato, Cucumber, Feta
    Cheese, and Greek Olives 45
Pasta Rings in Spicy Cucumber Raita 51
Pasta Shells with Crab Meat and West
    Coast Louis Dressing 72
Pasta with Fresh Basil Pesto 53
Pasta with Fresh Basil, Tomato, and
    Parmesan 43
Pasta with Fresh Corn and Lima Beans in
    Apple Cider Vinaigrette 58
Pasta with Fresh Fruits and Yogurt 86
Pasta with Gazpacho Dressing and
    Crunchy Vegetables 63

Pasta with Lobster in Tangy Tarragon
    Mayonnaise 34
Pasta with Muffuletta Olive Salad and
    Italian Meats 83
Pasta with Poached Meats and Vegetables
    in Garlic Aioli 79
Pasta with Smoked Salmon in Dill
    Dressing 36
Penne with Provencal Eggplant and Sweet
    Peppers 48
Poached Chicken Breast with Thai Peanut
    Sauce and Noodles 70
Saffron-Laced Pastina with Currants, Pine
    Nuts, and Mint 46
Spinach Pasta Primavera Verde 64
Vermicelli with Shrimp in Curried Yogurt
    76

CORN COOKBOOK:
Corn Salad 23

GRILL COOKBOOK:
Duck Breast with Red Wine Jelly 41

POTATO COOKBOOK:
All-American Potato Salad 31
Potato and Mussel Salad (Salade
    Francillon) 28
New Potato Salad in Red Onion Dressing
    26
Warm Crispy Potato Salad 66

RICE COOKBOOK:
Green Rice Salad 37
Spicy Rice and Shrimp Salad 39

SALMON COOKBOOK:
Salmon Salad Niçoise 70

SQUASH COOKBOOK:
Summer Garden Matchstick Salad 26

ACKNOWLEDGMENTS

All wooden salad plates, bowls, serving pieces, and accessories have been graciously provided by Vietri, importers of Italian tableware, available in fine stores throughout the United States and Canada.

Much of the flatware is from Fillamento, San Francisco.

Some of the backgrounds were provided by Clervi Marble, San Francisco; Dryden and Palmer Inc., Branford, CT; Granite and Marble World Trade, San Francisco; and Granite Construction/Felton Quarry, Santa Cruz, CA. Copper leaves on page 25 were prepared by James Wood, San Francisco.

Special thanks to my panel of recipe testers for their valued assistance and helpful comments:
Jan Ellis
Mary Ann Gilderbloom
Gail High
Jim Hildreth
Meri McEneny
Martha McNair
Marian May
Babs Retzer
John Richardson
Tom and Nancy Riess
Kristi Spence
Sabrina Vasquez
Kathryn Wittenmeyer

To Chronicle Books for suggesting this volume.

To Sharon Silva for her world-class copyediting.

To Ellen Berger-Quan for her invaluable assistance in the office, library, kitchen, and photography studio, as well as for her many shopping and schlepping expeditions.

To Jim Hildreth for teaching me to use the large format camera and for working with me so patiently to photograph this book.

To John Carr for letting me turn part of his house into a temporary photo studio and for arranging a special visit with Grandmother Carr.

To Cleve Gallat and Samantha Schwemler for once again transforming my design notions into book pages.

To my family and friends for providing continuous support and encouragement.

To Addie Prey, Buster Booroo, Joshua J. Chew, Michael T. Wigglebutt, and Dweasel Pickle for their loyalty during the project, although most salads rank far down their list of favorite foods.

To Lin Cotton for sticking by me through the ups and downs of my career and for treating me to a fantastic Polynesian birthday cruise at the conclusion of this manuscript.